PENGUIN BOOKS

WRITERS ON ORGANIZATIONS

Derek S. Pugh is Emeritus Professor of International Management at the Open University Business School. He is an Academician of the Academy of Learned Societies in the Social Sciences. He has also edited *Organization Theory: Selected Readings* (fourth edition, 1996) for Penguin.

David J. Hickson is Emeritus Professor of International Management and Organization at the Bradford University School of Management, England. He holds a Swedish Honorary Doctorate, is the first Honorary Fellow of the European Group for Organizational Studies, was a Fellow of the Netherlands Institute for Advanced Studies, and was Founding Editor-in-Chief of the international research journal *Organization Studies*. He has lectured at leading business schools worldwide.

The authors have also co-authored *Management Worldwide* (Penguin; new edition, 2002) and Professor Hickson has edited *Exploring Management Across the World* (Penguin, 1997), its companion volume.

Derek S. Pugh and David J. Hickson

Writers on Organizations

FIFTH EDITION

PENGUIN BOOKS

To our parents and to
our professional forebears

PENGUIN BOOKS

Published by the Penguin Group
Penguin Books Ltd, 80 Strand, London WC2R 0RL, England
Penguin Putnam Inc., 375 Hudson Street, New York, New York 10014, USA
Penguin Books Australia Ltd, 250 Camberwell Road, Camberwell, Victoria 3124, Australia
Penguin Books Canada Ltd, 10 Alcorn Avenue, Toronto, Ontario, Canada M4V 3B2
Penguin Books India (P) Ltd, 11 Community Centre, Panchsheel Park, New Delhi – 110 017, India
Penguin Books (NZ) Ltd, Cnr Rosedale and Airborne Roads, Albany, Auckland, New Zealand
Penguin Books (South Africa) (Pty) Ltd, 24 Sturdee Avenue, Rosebank 2196, South Africa

Penguin Books Ltd, Registered Offices: 80 Strand, London WC2R 0RL, England

www.penguin.com

First published by Hutchinson 1964
Second edition published in Penguin Books 1971
Third edition 1983
Fourth edition 1989
Fifth edition 1996

7

Set in 10/12 pt Monotype Bembo
Typeset by RefineCatch Limited, Bungay, Suffolk
Printed in England by Clays Ltd, St Ives plc

Contents

Introduction to the Fifth Edition

Since the first edition of this book appeared in 1964 it has been in gratifyingly continuous demand, having sold over a quarter of a million copies. With changing organizational issues and with new work making an impact, it is appropriate now to offer a fifth edition, once again completely revised. We have added descriptions of new writers, brought others up to date and made some rearrangement of the sections

It is a commonplace of discussion among managers and administrators that all organizations are different. Even so, it is important to study these differences and to classify them. Something useful can thus be said about various kinds of organizations, the ways in which they function and the behaviour of members within them. This book describes the contributions that many prominent writers have made to the understanding of organizations and their management.

In presenting these contributions, our aim has remained the same over the years. It is to give a direct introductory exposition of the views of leading authors whose ideas are currently the subject of interest and debate. We conceive of this work as a resource book giving a general overview of the field, and so we have not essayed critical analysis, which would be a quite different task. It is our hope that readers will bring their own critical appraisal to each contribution. Even so we are conscious of the very considerable selection and compression which is involved in presenting a writer's work in a few pages. Some distortions must inevitably result. We can only plead the best of intentions in that our hope is to entice the reader to go to the original listed sources in their richness and complexity. A fully revised edition of the companion volume *Organization Theory: Selected Readings* (edited by D. S. Pugh, Fourth edition, Penguin Books, 1997) presents extracts from the work of many of the writers summarized here.

One of the attractions of this introductory book is that it is a relatively slim volume. We have therefore had to balance the addition of new writers with the dropping of others. However, their contributions continue to form part of the flow of concepts and theories which nurture the field. We have therefore compiled an omnibus edition which contains the descriptions of all the writers included in all the previous editions of this book. This hardback volume, entitled *Great Writers on Organizations: The Omnibus Edition* by D. S. Pugh and D. J. Hickson (Dartmouth Publishing, 1993), will allow a fuller exploration of the subject.

In considering which changes to make in the present edition, we conducted a small informal survey of our professional colleagues in many countries of the world. We should like to thank them very much for responding so promptly with their views, which helped us in our deliberations. The decisions on content were, of course, ours alone.

Our heartfelt thanks go to our wives, who for the fifth time round suffered most in the cause.

Derek S. Pugh
Open University Business School,
1996

David J. Hickson
University of Bradford Management
Centre, 1996

ONE

The Structure of Organizations

The decisive reason for the advance of bureaucratic organization has always been its purely technical superiority over any other form of organization.
MAX WEBER

It may not be impossible to run an effective organization of 5,000 employees non-bureaucratically, but it would be so difficult that no one tries.
THE ASTON GROUP

The visible hand of managerial direction has replaced the invisible hand of market mechanisms in coordinating flows and allocating resources in major modern industries.
ALFRED D. CHANDLER

Transaction cost economizing is, we submit, the driving force that is responsible for the main institutional changes [in corporations].
OLIVER E. WILLIAMSON

Adhocracy [the innovative configuration] is the structure of our age.
HENRY MINTZBERG

Increasingly your corporations will come to resemble universities or colleges.
CHARLES HANDY

The task [of the transnational organization] is not to build a sophist-icated matrix structure, but to create a 'matrix in the minds of managers'.
CHRISTOPHER BARTLETT and SUMANTRA GHOSHAL

All organizations have to make provision for continuing activities directed towards the achievement of given aims. Regularities in activities such as task allocation, supervision and coordination are developed. Such regularities constitute the organization's structure, and the fact that these activities can be arranged in various ways means that organizations can have differing structures. Indeed, in some respects every organization is unique. But many writers have examined a variety of structures to see if any general principles can be extracted. This variety, moreover, may be related to variations in such factors as the objectives of the organization, its size, ownership, geographical location and technology of manufacture, which produce the characteristic differences in structure of a bank, a hospital, a mass production factory or a local government department.

The writers in this section are concerned to identify different forms of organizational structures and to explore their implications. Max Weber presents three different organizational types on the basis of how authority is exercised. He views one of these types – bureaucracy – as the dominant modern form. Derek Pugh and the Aston Group suggest that it is more realistic to talk in terms of dimensions of structures rather than types. Alfred Chandler shows how the management structure flows from the company strategy. Oliver E. Williamson points to the way in which the pressures on the organization to process its information efficiently leads to the type of relationship, market or hierarchical, which is developed. Henry Mintzberg describes a range of types of modern organizations and their effectiveness. Charles Handy identifies some established structures of organization, but suggests that a distinctively different new form is coming into being. Christopher Bartlett and Sumantra Ghoshal argue that for multinational firms to be successful in the current global market environment, they must develop an innovative new structure and culture of working.

All the contributors to this section suggest that an appropriate structure is vital to the efficiency of an organization and must be the subject of careful study in its own right.

Max Weber

Max Weber (1864–1920) was born in Germany. He qualified in law and then became a member of the staff of Berlin University. He remained an academic for the rest of his life, having a primary interest in the broad sweep of the historical development of civilizations through studies of the sociology of religion and the sociology of economic life. In his approach to both of these topics he showed a tremendous range in examining the major world religions, such as Judaism, Christianity and Buddhism, and in tracing the pattern of economic development from pre-feudal times. These two interests were combined in his classic studies of the impact of Protestant beliefs on the development of capitalism in Western Europe and the USA. Weber had the prodigious output and ponderous style typical of German philosophers, but those of his writings which have been translated into English have established him as a major figure in sociology.

Weber's principal contribution to the study of organizations was his theory of authority structures, which led him to characterize organizations in terms of the authority relations within them. This stemmed from a basic concern with why individuals obey commands, why people do as they are told. To deal with this problem Weber made a distinction between *power*, the ability to force people to obey, regardless of their resistance, and *authority*, where orders are voluntarily obeyed by those receiving them. Under an authority system, those in the subordinate role see the issuing of directives by those in the superordinate role as legitimate. Weber distinguished between organizational types according to the way in which authority is legitimized. He outlined three pure types, which he labelled 'charismatic', 'traditional' and 'rational–legal', each of which is expressed in a particular administrative apparatus or organization. These pure types are distinctions which are useful for analysing organizations, although any real organization may be a combination of them.

The first mode of exercising authority is based on the personal qualities of the leader. Weber used the Greek term *charisma* to mean any quality of individual personality by virtue of which the leader is set apart from ordinary people and treated as endowed with supernatural, superhuman or at least specifically exceptional powers or qualities. This is the position of the prophet, messiah or political leader, whose organization consists of a set of disciples: the disciples have the job of mediating between the leader and the masses. The typical case of this kind is a small-scale revolutionary movement either religious or political in form, but many organizations have had 'charismatic' founders, such as Lord Nuffield (Morris Motors) and Henry Ford. However, as the basis of authority is in the characteristics of one person and commands are based on that person's inspiration, this type of organization has a built-in instability. The question of succession always arises when the leader dies and the authority has to be passed on. Typically, in political and religious organizations the movement splits with the various disciples claiming to be the 'true' heirs to the charismatic leader. Thus the process is usually one of fission. The tendencies towards this kind of breakdown can be seen in the jockeying for position of Hitler's lieutenants, Himmler and Goering, during the first few months of 1945. It exemplifies the problem of an heir to the leader, and even if the leader nominates a successor, that person will not necessarily be accepted. It is unlikely that another charismatic leader will be present, and so the organization must lose its charismatic form, becoming one of the two remaining types. If the succession becomes hereditary, the organization becomes traditional in form; if the succession is determined by rules, a bureaucratic organization develops.

The bases of order and authority in *traditional* organizations are precedent and usage. The rights and expectations of various groups are established in terms of taking what has always happened as sacred; the great arbiter in such a system is custom. Leaders in such a system have authority by virtue of the status that they have inherited, and the extent of their authority is fixed by custom. When charisma is traditionalized by making its transmission hereditary, it becomes part of the role of the leader rather than being part of the founder's personality. The actual organizational form under a traditional authority system can take one of two patterns. There is the *patrimonial* form where officials are personal servants, dependent on the leader for remuneration. Under the *feudal* form the officials have much more autonomy with their own sources of income and a traditional relationship of loyalty towards the leader. The feudal system has a material basis of tithes, fiefs and beneficiaries, all resting on past usage and a system of customary rights and duties. Although Weber's examples are historical, his insight is equally applicable to modern organizations. Managerial positions are often handed down from one generation to the next as firms establish their own dynasties based on hereditary transmission. Selection and appointment may be based on kinship rather than expertise. Similarly, ways of doing things in many organizations are justified in terms of always having been done that way *as a reason in itself*, rather than on the basis of a rational analysis.

The concept of rational analysis leads to Weber's third type of authority system, the rational–legal one, with its bureaucratic organizational form. This Weber sees as the dominant institution of modern society. The system is called rational because the means are expressly designed to achieve certain specific goals (i.e. the organization is like a well designed machine with a certain function to perform, and every part of the machine contributes to the attainment of maximum performance of that function). It is legal because authority is exercised by means of a system of rules and procedures through the office which an individual occupies at a particular time. For such an organization Weber uses the name 'bureaucracy'. In common usage, bureaucracy is synonymous with inefficiency, an emphasis on red tape and excessive writing and recording. Specifically, it is identified with inefficient public administration. But in terms of his own definition, Weber states that a bureaucratic organization is technically the most efficient form of organization possible. 'Precision, speed, unambiguity, knowledge of files, continuity, discretion, unity, strict subordination, reduction of friction and of material and personal costs – these are raised to the optimum point in the strictly bureaucratic administration.' Weber himself uses the machine analogy when he says that the bureaucracy is like a modern machine, while other organizational forms are like non-mechanical methods of production.

The reason for the efficiency of the bureaucracy lies in its organizational form. As the means used are those which will best achieve the stated ends, it is unencumbered by the personal whims of the leader or by traditional procedures which are no longer applicable. This is because bureaucracies represent the final stage in depersonalization. In such organizations there is a series of officials, whose roles are circumscribed by written definitions of their authority. These offices are arranged in a hierarchy, each successive step embracing all those beneath it. There is a set of rules and procedures within which every possible contingency is theoretically provided for.

There is a 'bureau' for the safe keeping of all written records and files, it being an important part of the rationality of the system that information is written down. A clear separation is made between personal and business affairs, bolstered by a contractual method of appointment in terms of technical qualifications for office. In such an organization authority is based in the office, and commands are obeyed because the rules state that it is within the competence of a particular office to issue such commands. Also important is the stress on the appointment of experts. One of the signs of a developing bureaucracy is the growth of professional managers and an increase in the number of specialist experts with their own departments.

For Weber this adds up to a highly efficient system of coordination and control. The rationality of the organization shows in its ability to 'calculate' the consequences of its action. Because of the hierarchy of authority and the system of rules, control of the actions of individuals in the organization is assured; this is the depersonalization. Because of the employment of experts who have their specific areas of responsibility and the use of files, there is an amalgamation of the best available knowledge and a record of past behaviour of the organization. This enables predictions to be made about future events. The organization has rationality: 'the methodical attainment of a definitely given and practical end by means of an increasingly precise calculation of means'.

This is where the link between Weber's interest in religion and organizations occurs. Capitalism as an economic system is based on the rational long-term calculation of economic gain. Initially for this to happen, as well as the expansion of world markets, a particular moral outlook is needed. Weber saw this as being supplied by the Protestant religion after the Reformation with its emphasis on this world and the need for individuals to show their salvation through their industry on earth. Thus, economic activity gradually became labelled as a positive good rather than as a negative evil. Capitalism was launched on its path, and this path was cleared most easily through the organizational form of bureaucracy which supplied the apparatus for putting economic rationality into practice. Providing as it does efficiency and regularity, bureaucratic administration is a necessity for any long-term economic calculation. So with increasing industrialization, bureaucracy becomes the dominant method of organizing, and so potent is it that it becomes characteristic of other areas of society such as education, government, politics, etc. Finally, the bureaucratic organization becomes typical of all the institutions of modern society.

Most studies of the formal, structural characteristics of organizations over the past three decades have started from the work of Max Weber. His importance lies in having made the first attempt to produce systematic categories for organizational analysis.

BIBLIOGRAPHY

WEBER, M., *The Protestant Ethic and the Spirit of Capitalism*, Allen & Unwin, 1930.
WEBER, M., *The Theory of Social and Economic Organization*, Free Press, 1947.
GERTH, H. II., and MILLS, C. W. (eds.), *From Max Weber: Essays in Sociology*, Routledge & Kegan Paul, 1948.

Derek Pugh and the Aston Group, including John Child and David Hickson

In the 1950s Derek Pugh, now Visiting Research Professor of International Management at the Open University Business School, UK, brought to the Birmingham College of Advanced Technology (which became the University of Aston-in-Birmingham) a distinctive view of how to conduct research. His research experience as a social psychologist at the University of Edinburgh had placed him in close contact with researchers in other social sciences. He believed that the scope of empirical investigation and of understanding could be widened by multidisciplinary research, founded on a common commitment to and ownership of results within the research team, and on team management skills.

The Industrial Administration Research Unit at Aston, founded and led by Pugh between 1961 and 1970, included several 'generations' of researchers whose academic origins ranged from psychology, sociology, economics and politics, to no specific discipline at all. The names which appear most frequently on publications are John Child, David Hickson, Bob Hinings, Roy Payne, Diana Pheysey, and Charles McMillan as the initiator with David Hickson of much subsequent international research, but there are many more. It is symptomatic of the nature of the group that it has not taken on the name of any one individual, even that of Derek Pugh, but is usually known as the Aston Group, even though there is no longer any special link with that university. The programme of research dispersed with the members of the group, and they and others in touch with them have pursued its work elsewhere in Britain and in several other countries.

The Aston Programme contributed to organization theory by blending some of the research methods and assumptions of psychology with conceptions of organizations and their workings from sociology and economics. Its approach has three essential elements. First, because organizations and their members are changing and complex, numbers of their *attributes should be studied together and as matters of degree*, not as 'either/or' phenomena – a multi-variate approach to a changing world of greys, rather than blacks and whites. This also implies that there will be no single reason for the way in which an organization is set up and run, but many possible influences (i.e. multi-variate causal explanation). What happens cannot be due to an organization's size alone, nor for that matter to its technology alone, but must in some degree be due to a number of these and other factors all acting together.

Second, because organizations outlast the comings and goings of individuals, it is *appropriate to study their non-personal or institutional aspects* using information on their divisions of work, their control systems and their formal hierarchies. For this, individuals can be interviewed as informants who describe these aspects, rather than being asked to indicate how they experience the organization personally, which they would be if asked to respond to questionnaires about themselves.

Third, because organizations are working wholes, they and their members *should be seen from more than one perspective* to give the fullest possible view. 'The response to the recurring conundrum "does man make organization or does organization make man?" must be to assume that both are happening all the time.' Therefore, the Aston Programme aimed to link:

1. Organizational structure and functioning
2. Group composition and interaction
3. Individual personality and behaviour

Early ambitions to include features of the surrounding society were not realized initially, but began to be included later, when research extended beyond Britain to organizations in other societies.

The Programme commenced with a project in the Birmingham area in England, from which has grown all further research. It focused on the organizational level by studying a highly diverse sample of forty-six organizations: private sector and public sector, from manufacturers of cars and chocolate bars to municipal departments, public services and chain stores. Their formal structures were analysed in terms of their degrees of:

Specialization of functions and roles;
Standardization of procedures;
Formalization of documentation;

Centralization of authority;
Configuration of role structure.

These concepts reflect prevalent ideas about bureaucratization and how to manage, which can be found in the work of Weber (p. 5) and Fayol (p. 97).

A very large number of ways of measuring these aspects of structure were devised, which have been employed variously by many researchers since. The most distinctive kind of measure used, an innovation in research on organizations, was based on demonstrating that, for example, the number of functions (such as finance or public relations) that an organization had specialized out of a set of possible specialisms could validly be added to give it a specialization score, and similarly with standardization, formalization and centralization. This enabled one organization to be compared with another in these terms for the first time.

Despite the range and ramifications of this research, its salient results took on a relatively simple outline. First, the measures of specialization, standardization and formalization were simplified into a combined score for each organization. To distinguish this from its three constituents it was called *structuring of activities*. An organization with highly structured activities has many specialized sections such as buying, training, work study and so on, and many routine procedures and formal documents, the total effect being that what has to be done is marked out or structured. Second, centralization of decision-making and the autonomy of an organization's decision-making from any owning organization were together termed *concentration of authority*. An organization with concentrated authority not only has most of its decisions taken at the top of its own hierarchy but has many decisions taken for it, over its head, by the management of another organization of which it is a wholly or partly owned subsidiary or subordinate section.

Thus at its simplest, the Aston Group isolated two primary elements of any organization, how far the activities of its personnel are structured and how far its decision-making authority is concentrated at the top, which between them sum up much of what an organization is like. Know them and you know it, to a large extent, for they are its two fundamentals.

Although the Aston Programme's approach assumes that organizations are what they are for many reasons, these first results were also relatively simple in the principal explanations that they suggested. A series of features of the organizational context, including its purpose, ownership, technology, size and dependence, were examined for any correlation with how far an organization had structured its activities or concentrated its authority. It was found that ownership (whether private or public, dispersed in thousands of shareholdings or in the hands of a family) made little difference to structuring and concentration; as did technology, which was reflected in only a few aspects of structure.

What did and does matter much more for the form taken by an organization is its *size*, and its degree of *dependence upon other organizations*. The larger it is, the more likely its employees are to work in very specialized functions, following standardized procedures and formalized documentation; that is, it will score highly on structuring of activities and have many of the appearances of bureaucracy. The more it is dependent upon only a few owning, supplier or customer units, or even just one – total dependence is where an organization is wholly owned by another which supplies all its needs and takes all its outputs – the less autonomy it will have in its own decision-making, and even those decisions that are left to it are likely to be centralized within itself rather than decentralized.

Casting its results into an empirically derived taxonomy of forms of organization structure, the Aston Group put forward from its first project a view of the forms prevalent in contemporary industrialized society, in Britain and probably elsewhere too. Large firms and big businesses are typically *workflow bureaucracies*, highly structured but not as highly concentrated in authority as some. Public service organizations of local and central government are *personnel bureaucracies*, not very structured but with highly concentrated authority and procedures focused on the hiring, promoting and firing of personnel. Smaller units within large private or public groups are *full bureaucracies*, with the high structuring of the workflow type and the highly concentrated authority of the personnel type. Smaller firms in personal ownership have neither of these features to any great extent, being *non-bureaucracies* (or implicitly structured). There are other types, but these four main ones can be depicted as on the next page.

The progression of the Aston Group into research on group and role characteristics and on the individual's experience of organizational 'climate', in accordance with their Programme of linking organizational, group and individual levels of analysis, is not so well known. Its results are not so clear cut. If any construction can be placed on them overall, it is that they lift from bureaucracy the pall of gloom laid over it by widespread

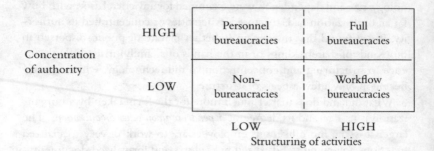

assumptions of its uniformly stifling and dreary nature. It may be like that: but if it is, then it is for those in the lowest-level jobs and not necessarily for those higher in the hierarchy. Life for them differs from one bureaucratic organization to another.

Through a mixture of surveys and of intensive case studies with batteries of methods, Aston researchers showed that while structuring of activities does tend to be associated with greater formality at the group interaction level, and concentration of authority does tend to be associated with less autonomy for individuals and with greater conventional attention to rules, nevertheless a uniformly bureaucratic-type firm can be effective and its personnel can like working in it. At least, this was so in their case study of a small firm owned by a large international corporation, a 'small effective bureaucracy' which they code-named 'Aston'.

In organizations that showed both high structuring and high concentration of authority, which were loosely equated with bureaucracies, there was no evidence of less attractive 'climates' (in terms of the way in which authority was exercised, of interest in work, of routine and of personal relationships). At the top, such organizations tended to have managers who were younger and better qualified, with more flexible and challenging attitudes. And firms with younger managers tended to show faster growth in sales and assets (though whether youth caused growth or growth attracted younger personnel is an unanswered question). So those managing more bureaucratic-type firms were unlikely themselves to be cautious and conformist, and were more likely to seek innovation and risk.

Greater confidence is shown in the Aston Programme's achievements at the organizational level of analysis, however. On issues such as the presence or absence of procedures, documents, defined authority and control systems, the Programme demonstrated that significant comparisons can be made between organizations of virtually any kind. (But it must be remembered that the data do not tell how far these means are then used.) The Aston Programme provides concepts and measures of organizational structure that have withstood use and re-use by researchers beyond the original team in a way that rarely happens.

JOHN CHILD

John Child, now Guinness Professor of Management at the Judge Institute of Management Studies at the University of Cambridge, joined Pugh at Aston in using the same methods to replicate the results in contrasting industries, stable compared to fast changing.

Most significantly, he made explicit what had remained implicit in the thinking behind the Aston Programme. He highlighted *strategic choice* by emphasizing that all aspects of organizations were in some sense chosen by their managements. They did not just happen. Size, for example, does not 'cause' specialization just like that. Growth in size enables, or pressures, managers who want to have effective organizations to add more specialist departments so that work can be divided clearly between more people, who thus acquire more specialized expertise. It is the managers who choose what to do. More than that, they choose the growth in size to begin with. They decide to expand output, add a new marketing department, or whatever, and so they increase the numbers of employees. Strategic choice by managers affects both context and structure.

But *one choice constrains another* – each choice (e.g. of size) constrains the options open for the next (e.g. of the degree of structuring to be adopted). A major instance of this is that the choice of how far to develop either of the two primary elements, structuring and concentration, is likely to limit to some extent what can be done with the other, for there is a small negative relationship between them; that is, more of one probably means somewhat less of the other, and to that extent they are alternative means of controlling an organization – not mutually exclusive alternatives (since all organizations use both) but alternative emphases.

Later Child spent some years in China during the transition from Maoist rule. In some of the first ever independent empirical research in that nation's industries, he and Chinese colleagues exposed the problems of devolving a centrally planned system. Decentralization was uneven and only partially effective. Central and local government kept capital investment in their own hands, and formal delegation to managements of decisions on, for instance, purchasing and recruiting, meant little if in practice managers had to go to state agencies to find sources of goods and personnel.

DAVID HICKSON

David Hickson, now Research Professor of International Management at Bradford Management Centre, England, who was with the Aston Group from the beginning, shared with Pugh a particular responsibility for extending its work beyond Britain. Over the years, Aston-based projects took place in many nations worldwide, including the United States and Canada, Western Europe, together with Poland and Sweden, the Middle East and Israel, India, Hong Kong, and Japan. Among the differences which have been found are notably high centralization of organizations under state central planning in Poland, high structuring (specialization and formalization) in Japanese companies which have adopted contemporary Western forms of organization and management, and comparatively less structuring in paternalistic Hong Kong firms.

Hickson, Hinings and colleagues put forward a *culture-free hypothesis*, which originated from a comparison of manufacturing firms in Britain, Canada and the United States. As they saw it, this stated the 'boldest' possibility, namely: 'Relationships between the structural characteristics of work organizations and variables of organization context will be stable across societies.' Greater size, for instance, would consistently go with greater specialization and greater formalization, in any country, West or East. Lex Donaldson of the Australian Graduate School of Management in Sydney, a former colleague of Pugh's at the London Business School and once a student of Hickson's at Aston itself, is a constant advocate of the kind of work accomplished by the Aston Group. He tested this hypothesis using the published results of studies in thirteen countries across the world and found that it was supported. There were indeed stable relationships, especially with size of organization. Everywhere bigger organizations are not only likely to be more structured, but also less centralized (the latter relationship may be weaker in the East). In other words, once jobs and procedures are set up, top managers can delegate more because people know what they should do, and simultaneously they ask to be allowed to do it. This finding suggests not that all organizations are the same, but that managers in all nations have similar constraints upon their choices, which show up as a repeated pattern of relationships between size, and dependence, and structural features.

Again with Hinings, and with other colleagues in the Faculty of Business at the University of Alberta, Canada, Hickson went on to examine which managers most influence these choices, and why. They proposed a *strategic contingencies theory of intraorganizational power*, building up the ideas of Crozier (p. 151), and verified it by studying departmental influence in firms in Canada and the United States. The theory gives three reasons why some departmental managers are powerful and others weak. These are how far they *cope with uncertainty*, are *centrally situated* and are *not substitutable*. If their department can cope with uncertainty, then the rest of the organization can function with fewer difficulties, as when a marketing department evens out erratic fluctuations in customer demands by astute advertising, so that production can be more stable year-round. If their department is central to the flows of work around the organization, then more of the others who feed work to it and wait upon its work are dependent upon it, as when a finance department receives estimates and allocates budgets. If this department cannot be substituted for, since no one else in the organization nor any external agency can do what it does, then it holds a monopoly-like position. Should there be an alternative, as when some of the work of a purchasing department could be contracted out to a buying agent, that position is fragile.

Departmental managers whose personnel is strong in all three respects have an overall *control of strategic contingencies* within their organization that gives them more influence over decisions than anyone else has, even over decisions outside their departmental concerns. Pfeffer and Salancik (p. 71) used this same idea in their theory about an organization's external relationships.

Hickson, together with colleagues at Bradford Management Centre, then investigated how these managerial decisions, particularly the major ones, came to be made. Comparing 150 histories of decisions in thirty organizations in England, they found three prevalent ways of making such decisions. Decisions could be arrived at by a process that was *sporadic*, 'informally spasmodic and protracted', or *fluid*, 'steadily paced, formally channelled, speedy', or *constricted*, 'narrowly channelled'.

Which type of process occurred depended more on what was being decided than on the kind of organization, manufacturer or hospital or utility or whatever it might be, in which it was being decided. The most complex and political matters (which could be new products or major reorganizations, for example) most often gave rise to a sporadic process; those that were still complex but less political (which could be a big share issue, for example) were likely to go through a smoother, fluid process; whilst those that were still political but less complex (which could be the organization's corporate budget and business plan) were likely to go through a tighter, constricted process. As the Bradford researchers put it, 'the matter for decision matters most.'

Together with his colleagues, Hickson therefore draws attention to three of the more crucial features of what managers have to work with. First, wherever in the world they may be, there will be consistent constraints, one decision upon another, in the structural features – as defined by the Aston Programme – that characterize organizations. Second, they must expect differing patterns of influence in different organizations – marketing may have great say in one firm but little in another, for instance. Third, by contrast, they will be able to recognize what is going on when big decisions are made in organizations other than their own, easily fitting in if they change jobs – a similarly complex and political matter is likely to engender much the same process wherever it occurs.

BIBLIOGRAPHY

Aston Programme Books:

PUGH, D. S., and HICKSON, D. J., *Organizational Structure in Its Context: The Aston Programme I*, Gower Publishing, 1976.

PUGH, D. S., and HININGS, C. R. (eds.), *Organizational Structure – Extensions and Replications: The Aston Programme II*, Gower Publishing, 1976.

PUGH, D. S., and PAYNE, R. L. (eds.), *Organizational Behaviour in Its Context: The Aston Programme III*, Gower Publishing, 1977.

HICKSON, D. J., and MCMILLAN, C. J. (eds.), *Organization and Nation: The Aston Programme IV*, Gower Publishing, 1981.

Aston Programme Further Papers:

CHILD, J., 'Organizational Structures, Environment and Performance: the Role of Strategic Choice', *Sociology* 6 (1972), 2–22.

PUGH, D. S., 'The Measurement of Organization Structures: Does Context Determine Form?', *Organizational Dynamics* (Spring 1973), 19–34; reprinted in D. S. Pugh (ed.), *Organization Theory*, Penguin, 1997.

DONALDSON, L., 'Size and Bureaucracy in East and West: A Preliminary Meta Analysis', in S. R. Clegg, D. C. Dunphy and S. G. Redding, *The Enterprise and Management in East Asia*, University of Hong Kong, 1986.

Further Work:

HICKSON, D. J., HININGS, C. R., LEE, C. A., SCHNECK, R. E., and PENNINGS, J. M., 'A Strategic Contingencies Theory of Intraorganizational Power', *Administrative Science Quarterly*, 16/2 (1971), 216–29.

HININGS, C. R., HICKSON, D. J., PENNINGS, J. M., and SCHNECK, R. C., 'Structural Conditions of Intraorganizational Power', *Administrative Science Quarterly*, 19/1 (1974), 22–44.

DONALDSON, L., *In Defence of Organization Theory*, Cambridge University Press, 1985.

HICKSON, D. J., BUTLER, R. J., CRAY, D., MALLORY, G. R., and WILSON, D. C., *Top Decisions*, Blackwell and Jossey-Bass, 1986.

CHILD, J., *Management in China during the Age of Reform*, Cambridge University Press, 1994.

DONALDSON, L., *American Anti-Management Theories of Organization*, Cambridge University Press, 1995.

Alfred D. Chandler

Alfred Chandler is Straus Professor of Business History in the Graduate School of Business Administration, Harvard University. He is an economic historian and his research work has centred on the study of business history and, in particular, administration. He has long argued that this is a much neglected area in the study of recent history. His studies of big business have been carried out with grants from a number of sources, including the Alfred P. Sloan Foundation. His work has been internationally recognized, and his book *The Visible Hand* was awarded the Pulitzer Prize for History and the Bancroft Prize. Chandler has taught at a variety of universities in the United States and Europe.

All of Chandler's academic work has been concerned with the theme of the rise and role of the large-scale business enterprise during what he describes as the formative years of modern capitalism. These are the years 1850–1920. He suggests, from his many studies, that during this period a new economic institution was created, the multi-unit firm, controlled by a new class of managers operating within a new system of capitalism. These new managers had to develop strategies different from those of their entrepreneurial predecessors and be particularly innovative in creating structures to implement those strategies. The reasons for this shift are to be found in changes in demand bringing about mass markets and technological change which allowed high-volume production. The new organization structures allowed the integration of mass production with mass distribution.

While Chandler's analysis is historical, he makes general points about organizational change and the relationship between strategy and structure. In particular, from his studies, Chandler is clear that the structure of an organization follows from the strategy that is adopted. The distinction between these two is crucial. *Strategy* is the determination of basic long-term goals and objectives together with the adoption of courses of action and the allocation of resources for carrying out those goals. *Structure* is the organization which is devised to administer the activities which arise from the strategies adopted. As such it involves the existence of a hierarchy, the distribution of work and lines of authority and communication. In addition, the concept of structure covers the information and data that flow along those lines.

Once an organization moves away from the small, owner-controlled enterprise towards the modern, multi-unit business enterprise, then the new class of managers appears. This is important for structural developments because the salaried manager is committed to the long-term stability of the enterprise. The managerial hierarchy gives positions of power and authority and as a result becomes a source both of permanence and continued growth. As part of this process the careers of salaried managers become increasingly technical and professional.

The role of management in developing structure is central to Chandler's analysis. As he puts it, 'the visible hand of management has replaced Adam Smith's invisible hand of market forces.' Managers are both products of, and developers of, the multi-divisional, decentralized structure which is the organizational outcome of technological change and rising demand. They become responsible for the administration of the enterprise, that is, coordinating, planning and appraising work, and allocating resources.

The structural arrangements of a large business enterprise have to allow both for the efficient day-to-day operations of its various units and for dealing with the long-run health of the company. The developments which follow from this involve operating with a decentralized structure to deal with day-to-day manufacturing and services, and building up a central office with functional departments to manage the long-run prospects of the company. This is all part of the process of specialization of functions as a major structural device. The key distinctions are between the general office, divisions, departments and field units. Each of these has a particular function and one of the basic reasons for the success of this type of structure is that it clearly removed from the immediate operations those executives responsible for long-term planning and appraisal. The significance of this separation is that it gives those executives the time, information and psychological commitment for long-term activities.

The introduction of this distinctive organizational structure with its unique managerial hierarchy marked the transition from a family- or finance-based capitalism to managerial capitalism. But because, in Chandler's view, structure follows strategy, this transition could only occur in response to external pressures. Particularly important was the increasing volume of activity which arose in response to the new national and increasingly urban markets of the late nineteenth century. Together with this was the technological change which enabled enterprises to move into high-volume production.

In the face of such pressures, enterprises could adopt either defensive or positive strategies. A *positive strategy* occurs when an enterprise actively looks for new markets and new products to serve those markets. It is organized around product diversification. A *defensive strategy* is where an enterprise acts to protect its current position. The common way of achieving this is to form a vertically integrated company by means of mergers with similar enterprises, suppliers and customers.

Both strategies lead to bigger organizations which have administrative problems. This begins a systematization of techniques for the administration of functional activities. An initial type of organization for achieving this is the centralized, functionally departmentalized structure. It enables the necessary, new expert skills to be brought in but retains control by the owners. But the increase in scale of organizations involves building up capacity and enlarging the resources of people, money and materials at the disposal of an enterprise. A result of this is further and continuing growth to ensure the full use of those resources, a result which emanates from the interests of the new managers rather than the owners. Growth becomes internally as well as externally generated and then produces the really innovative structure, that of the multi-unit decentralized form.

To illustrate his points in detail and to chart the process of structural innovation, Chandler looks at the cases of four companies: Du Pont, General Motors, Standard Oil of New Jersey and Sears Roebuck. According to Chandler, the general pressures and needs facing these four companies were the same. Also in general terms, the structural outcome was very similar. But the process of diagnosing the issues and introducing the consequent administrative changes was quite different.

The particular structural innovation of Du Pont was to create autonomous divisions. The company reached the beginning of the twentieth century as a loose federation with no central administrative control. The first strategy of the younger Du Ponts was to centralize control and concentrate manufacturing activity in a few, larger plants. This was the centralized, functionally departmentalized structure. Important to the operation of the company was the development of new forms of management information and forecasting. The introduction of the multi-unit, decentralized structure came with the need to maintain growth. It was done by basing the structure on a new principle, coordinating related effort rather than like things. This innovative principle meant that different broad functional activities had to be placed in separate administrative units. To operate these units, the executives responsible were given enhanced authority. Eventually these developed into product-based units backed by a central, general office to deal with strategic issues. This left the autonomous units to get on with day-to-day operations.

The General Motors case underlines the need for structure to follow strategy. William Durant, the founder of General Motors, went for a volume strategy with many operating units in an extremely loose federation. There was a crisis in 1920 due to lack of overall control. The response of Alfred P. Sloan, who became the Chief Executive Officer in 1923, was to create a general office to be responsible for broad policies and objectives and to coordinate effort. A line-and-staff structure was developed, allowing the product divisions to ensure good use of resources and a proper product flow, with the headquarters staff appraising divisional performance and plans. The new structure took five years to put in place.

Sloan has described in *My Years with General Motors* the nature of the problems and the need for changes as he saw them from the Chief Executive's point of view. Top management has the basic tasks of providing motivation and opportunity for its senior executives; motivation by incentive compensation through stock option plans, and opportunity through decentralized management. But coordination is also required, and good management rests on a reconciliation of centralization and decentralization. It was through his attempts to obtain the correct structural balance between these extremes that Sloan enunciated his seemingly paradoxical principle of 'coordinated decentralization'. His aim was co-ordinated control of decentralized operations. Policy coordination is achieved through committees. It is evolved in a continuous debate to which all may contribute, and is basically an educational process. Executive administration is the clear responsibility of individuals who carry out the evolving policy.

As with General Motors, Standard Oil of New Jersey was, for Chandler, a case of initial failure to adjust structure to strategy. The channels of authority and communication were insufficiently defined within a partly federated, partly consolidated company. As a result there was a series of crises over inventories and over-production during the 1920s which led to *ad hoc* responses. The initial development was to build up a central office for resource allocation and coordination. A second stage was to set up a decentralized divisional structure. According to Chandler, the response in Standard Oil was slower and more tentative than in Du Pont or General Motors partly because the problems were more difficult and partly because of a general lack of concern with organizational problems.

During the 1920s and 1930s, Sears Roebuck underwent the same process in its own particular way, partly planned and partly unplanned. The initial defensive strategy of vertical integration produced a centralized, functionally departmentalized structure. Continued growth produced the pressure for decentralized, regional organization and for sorting out the relationships between operating units and functional departments. Contributors to the book edited by Chandler and Daems trace similar processes in French, German and British industry.

For Chandler, both his case studies and his broader work illustrate a number of general points about structural development and organizational innovation. The first is that the market and technological pressures of an urban, industrial society push enterprises in the same structural direction, but the actual process of innovation can be quite different. In this process it is important to distinguish between an adaptive response and a creative innovation. An *adaptive response* is a structural change which stays within the range of current custom and practice, as was the case with functional departments and a central office. A *creative innovation* goes beyond existing practice and procedures, developing decentralized field units, for example. The general adoption of a line-and-staff departmental structure meant that delegation of authority and responsibility to field units was possible.

From this process, says Chandler, there arises a new economic function in society, that of administrative coordination and control. To carry out that function, a new species is created, the salaried manager. In carrying out the function the modern business enterprise is produced, with its two specific characteristics – the existence of many distinct operating units and their management by a hierarchy of salaried executives.

BIBLIOGRAPHY

CHANDLER, A. D., *Strategy and Structure*, MIT Press, 1962.

CHANDLER, A. D., *The Visible Hand: The Managerial Revolution in American Business*, Harvard University Press, 1977.

CHANDLER, A. D., and DAEMS, H. (eds.), *Managerial Hierarchies: Comparative Perspectives on the Rise of Modern Industrial Enterprises*, Harvard University Press, 1980.

CHANDLER, A. D., and TEDLOW, R. S., *The Coming of Managerial Capitalism*, Irwin, 1985.

SLOAN, A. P., *My Years with General Motors*, Sidgwick & Jackson, 1965.

Oliver E. Williamson

Oliver Williamson, an American economist, began his working life as a project engineer in US government service, but soon moved into academic life, taking degrees at the universities of Stanford and Carnegie-Mellon. His career has taken him through leading American universities and he is now TransAmerica Professor of Business, Economics and Law at the University of California, Berkeley.

Williamson probes beneath the usual questions about what organizations are like and how their members behave to ask why they are there at all. Why organizations? His answer is because they lower the cost of transactions. He sees society as a network of transactions − contracts in the widest sense of that term − and suggests that a 'transactional paradigm' will yield the reasons for organizations. These reasons are not size − that is, the economies of scale which have been supposed to explain large organizations − nor large-scale technologies, but the information cost of transactions. Size and technology are important not in themselves but because of the demands they make for information.

Each of the multitude of recurrent transactions which take place in a society can be conducted either in a market or within an organization. Which mode of transacting is used depends upon the information available and the costs to the transacting parties of adding to that information should they require more. So as the requirements for information change, transactions may be conducted more in markets, or more and more within organizations. The trend has been for more transactions to be gathered within the boundaries of organizations, and Williamson's discussion is primarily about change in that direction. That is because he has been concerned mainly with societies moving that way, but if the starting point were a society in which central planning and non-market transactions predominated, the analysis could as appropriately deal with the shifting of transactions from within organizations out to markets. Analysis of transaction costs can answer 'why not organizations?' as well as 'why organizations?'

Williamson's point of view joins market economics to organization theory in a form of institutional economics. He looks forward to the possibility that measures of market structure will eventually combine with measures of the internal structure of organizations (see Derek Pugh and the Aston Group, p. 10).

Markets and *hierarchies* are alternatives for conducting transactions. So transactions are brought within the hierarchical structures of organizations when the market mode is no longer efficient. For example, mergers or takeovers bring into a single organization contracting parties whose transactions will then be regulated by the internal rules of a hierarchy and not by the rules of a market. Or organizations are set up to transact within themselves business that might alternatively have been done by separate parties contracting between themselves in market terms.

Which mode is adopted depends upon the degree of *information impactedness*. This exists when the 'true underlying circumstances' of a transaction are known to one or more parties but not to others. Where there is less than complete trust between the parties, those who lack information could only obtain parity by incurring costs, which may be high, even prohibitive. Thus a buyer who is offered supplies may be unsure whether the quality will be what is required, whether delivery is likely to be on time, or how far the proposed price is more than need be paid. This may be because no one, not even the seller, has adequate information on these matters; or it may be that even if information is available, the buyer cannot trust it because the seller will have interpreted it to favour the selling vantage point.

A market is the most efficacious mode of conducing transactions when all necessary information is conveyed between parties by a price, and this single item of information is sufficient. Transactions are better brought within a hierarchy when much more must be known, much less is certain, and there may be 'quasi-moral' elements, for the hierarchy brings the inadequately informed parties to a transaction together under some degree of control.

Transactions will be shifted out of a market and into the hierarchy of a firm, or other form of organization, when information impactedness is high, that is, when the uncertainties and distrust inherent in transactions become too great for prices to be acceptably determined. At this point the advantages of hierarchy become the greater. First, it extends the bounds on rationality. Though the rationalities of each of the parties within an organization are still restricted, specialization enables each to deal with a part of the overall problem that is small enough to be comprehended, the results of the work of them all being brought together by specialized decision-makers at the apex. More information is exchanged or can be required to be handed over. Common numbering and coding systems and occupational jargon cut down communication costs. Second, sub-sections of an organization can each attend to a given aspect of the uncertainty-complexity of a situation, so making manageable a problem which would in total be too uncertain-complex. Aspects can be attended to as the situation unfolds, rather than all at once, and decisions which might otherwise be too complex can be split down into smaller sequential steps (see March, p. 139). Third, a hierarchy curbs opportunism. Pay, promotion, and control techniques ensure that the parties work in some degree towards common goals. Confidence may not be complete but it is greater. Parties cannot use their gains entirely for their own ends, and what they do can be more effectively checked and audited. Should disputes arise, superior hierarchical levels can decide them. Fourth, where there are small numbers, a situation which opportunistic parties are inclined to take advantage of, the hierarchy can overrule bargaining.

In general then, hierarchy more nearly approaches parity of information, and in particular, provides for quasi-moral and reciprocal obligations over and above strictly economic ones.

What then stops hierarchies taking over more and more transactions indefinitely? The limits begin to appear as firms grow larger and as vertical integration between firms extends. Costs then rise to a level at which the marginal costs of administering the incremental transaction begin to exceed those of completing transactions through a market. The goals of groups or sub-sections within an organization start to outweigh the common aims, the proliferation of specialists in control systems to combat this tendency becomes more and more expensive, sunk costs encourage the persistence of existing ways of doing things even if they would not now be done that way, were they to be started afresh, and communication is increasingly distorted. Leaders become more distant from those they lead – 'bureaucratic insularity' – and cooperation between those at lower levels becomes perfunctory rather than wholehearted. Coordination and common purpose lapse.

These costs rise in the unitary structure of hierarchy (called U-form), when the top management of the single large organization tries to control transactions within it. The U-form is therefore a vanishing breed among large US corporations, although the Reynolds Metal Company and the Quaker Oats Company retained this form right throughout the 1960s. Organizational transaction costs can be relatively reduced by the adoption of a multi-divisional structure (called M-form) as in the examples described by Chandler (see p. 22) of Du Pont, General Motors, Standard Oil of New Jersey and Sears Roebuck, who changed to the M-form in the twenties and thirties. To be effective, this form of organization requires a general overall management which concentrates on monitoring the performance of the constituent divisions and on strategic planning. Management can use the multi-divisional structure as a miniature capital market in which funds are moved into the most profitable uses more effectively than by the external capital market, because internally there is more complete information about the firm than parties in the external capital market have about comparative investment opportunities.

But if general management gets involved in the day-to-day operation of the divisions, then information costs will be again forced up, in what is called the 'corrupted M-form'. One large corporation is quoted as attempting to move from the corrupted M-form by releasing a total of 5,000 non-production personnel. It also reduced corporate staff – people not reporting to profit centres – by over 1,300, down to a new total of 132. The aim was to decentralize into true profit centres in which each divisional manager's performance could be accurately evaluated without the allocation of heavy corporate overheads.

If the change from the corrupted M-form cannot be achieved and the information costs remain high, then market transactions will become more attractive. For ultimately it is the relative cost of overcoming information impactedness that determines whether the transactions in a society are conducted through markets or within organizations.

BIBLIOGRAPHY

WILLIAMSON, O. E., *Markets and Hierarchies: Analysis and Antitrust Implications*, Free Press, 1975.
WILLIAMSON, O. E., *Economic Organization*, Wheatsheaf Books, 1986.

Henry Mintzberg

Henry Mintzberg is Bronfman Professor of Management at McGill University, Montreal. He graduated from the Sloan School of Management at the Massachusetts Institute of Technology. Among a variety of consulting assignments and visiting appointments, he has been visiting professor at the University of Aix-en-Provence in France. He has studied what managers actually do as they manage, and what kinds of organization they are managing.

Mintzberg shows a substantial difference between what managers do and what they are said to do. On the basis of work activity studies, he demonstrates that a manager's job is characterized by pace, interruptions, brevity, variety and fragmentation of activities and a preference for verbal contacts. Managers spend a considerable amount of time in scheduled meetings and in networks of contacts outside meetings.

The fragmentary nature of what managers do leads to the suggestion that they have to perform a wide variety of roles. Mintzberg suggests that there are ten managerial roles which can be grouped into three areas: *interpersonal, informational* and *decisional*.

Interpersonal roles cover the relationships that a manager has to have with others. The three roles within this category are figurehead, leader and liaison. Managers have to act as *figureheads* because of their formal authority and symbolic position, representing their organizations. As *leaders*, managers have to bring together the needs of an organization and those of the individuals under their command. The third interpersonal role, that of *liaison*, deals with the horizontal relationships which work-activity studies have shown to be important for a manager. A manager has to maintain a network of relationships outside the organization.

Managers have to collect, disseminate and transmit information and have three corresponding informational roles, namely monitor, disseminator and spokesperson. A manager is an important figure in *monitoring* what goes on in the organization, receiving information about both internal and external events and transmitting it to others. This process of transmission is the *dissemination* role, passing on information of both a factual and value kind. A manager often has to give information concerning the organization to outsiders, taking on the role of *spokesperson* to both the general public and those in positions of influence.

As with so many writers about management, Mintzberg regards the most crucial part of managerial activity as that concerned with making decisions. The four roles that he places in this category are based on different classes of decision, namely, entrepreneur, disturbance handler, resource allocator and negotiator. As *entrepreneurs*, managers make decisions about changing what is happening in an organization. They may have to both initiate change and take an active part in deciding exactly what is to be done. In principle, they are acting voluntarily. This is very different from their role as a *disturbance handler*, where managers have to make decisions which arise from events beyond their control and unpredicted. The ability to react to events as well as to plan activities is an important managerial skill in Mintzberg's eyes.

The *resource allocation* role of a manager is central to much organizational analysis. Clearly a manager has to make decisions about the allocation of money, people, equipment, time and so on. Mintzberg points out that in doing so a manager is actually scheduling time, programming work and authorizing actions. The *negotiation* role is put in the decisional category by Mintzberg because it is 'resource trading in real time'. A manager has to negotiate with others and in the process be able to make decisions about the commitment of organizational resources.

For Mintzberg these ten roles provide a more adequate description of what managers do than any of the various schools of management thought. In these roles it is information that is crucial; the manager is determining the priority of information. Through the interpersonal roles a manager acquires information, and through the decisional roles it is put into use.

The scope for each manager to choose a different blend of roles means that management is not reducible to a set of scientific statements and programmes. Management is essentially an art and it is necessary for managers to try and learn continuously about their own situations. Self-study is vital. At the moment there is no solid basis for teaching a theory of managing. According to Mintzberg, 'the management school has been more

Seven Organizational Types			
Organizational Configuration	*Prime Coordinating Mechanism*	*Key Part*	*Type of Decentralization*
Entrepreneurial	Direct supervision	Strategic apex	Vertical and horizontal centralization
Machine	Standardization of work processes	Technostructure	Limited horizontal decentralization
Professional	Standardization of skills	Operating core	Horizontal decentralization
Diversified	Standardization of outputs	Middle line	Limited vertical decentralization
Innovative	Mutual adjustment	Support staff	Selected decentralization
Missionary	Standardization of norms	Ideology	Decentralization
Political	None	None	Varies

from Mintzberg (1989)

effective at training technocrats to deal with structured problems than managers to deal with unstructured ones.'

Mintzberg presents a way of understanding the design of organizations and suggests that there are seven types. As shown in the table, the first five types are differentiated according to which basic part of the organization forms the key to its operations. In the entrepreneurial organization it is the strategic apex which is key. In a manufacturer, for example, this would be the President or Chief Executive, the Board of Directors, and their personal staff. In a machine organization, it is the 'technostructure' which is key: this includes those in planning, finance, training, operations research and work study, and production scheduling. The key part in a professional organization is the 'operating core', those at the working base of the organization. While in a manufacturer this would be the buyers, machine operators, salespeople and despatchers, in a professional organization it might be doctors and nurses (in a hospital) or teaching staff (in a college). The 'middle line' are key in the diversified organization, being the personnel who 'manage managers' in the hierarchy between the strategic apex and the operating core. In manufacturing these would include the heads of the production and sales functions and the managers and supervisors beneath them. In an innovative organization which Mintzberg calls an 'adhocracy' the 'support staff' are the key part. In a typical manufacturer they might be in public relations, industrial relations, pricing, payroll, even the cafeteria, as well as in research and development, but in an adhocracy the focus is upon the latter, the 'R & D'. In the final two configurations, no part of the organization itself is key. Missionary organizations are pulled by ideology, and political organizations have no key feature.

In each of the first five types, its key part exerts a 'pull' upon the organization. 'To the extent that conditions favour one over the others, the organization is drawn to structure itself as one of the configurations,' or designs. It is pulled towards one more than towards the others

The first type, the *entrepreneurial organization*, in which the strongest pull is by the *strategic apex* towards centralization, is as simple as its name indicates. It has little or no technostructure, few support staff, minimal differentiation between departments and a small hierarchy. Coordination is by direct supervision, downwards from the strong apex where power is in the hands of the Chief Executive: so it does not need formal planning or training or similar procedures, and can be flexible and 'organic' (see also Burns, p. 53). The conditions favouring this form are those of the classic entrepreneurial owner-managed firm. A small organization is a simple yet dynamic environment which can be understood by one leading individual. Most organizations pass through this structure in their formative years, and some stay small enough to continue it. They could be as diverse as an automobile dealership, a retail store, a brand-new government department or a vigorous manufacturer on a small scale.

Some people enjoy working in such an organization because of the sense of mission it gives, and its flexibility. Others resent the domination from the top. They see it as paternalistic or autocratic, unfashionable in democratic times. The organization is also precarious: 'one heart attack can literally wipe out the organization's prime coordinating mechanism.'

The *machine organization* is far more secure (see Weber on bureaucracy,

p. 7). It does not depend on a single person. The strongest pull on it is from its *technostructure*, the planners, financial controllers, production schedulers, and their kind. They pull towards standardization. Once work has been divided into standard routine tasks it can be controlled by them through formalized rules and regulations. Control is almost an obsession. It is second only to the entrepreneurial structure in centralization, but in it power is divided between the strategic apex and the technostructure. A post office, a steel manufacturer, a prison, a major airline, a vehicle assembler, are all like this. They have the conditions favouring this design, mainly that they are older, larger organizations carrying out repetitive work in stable environments, probably themselves subject to control from a remote corporation head office or government.

Though efficient at repetitive work, this form of organization is riddled with conflict between top and bottom and between departments. To many of its personnel the work they do is meaningless. Its managers spend much of their energy just holding it together. It was fashionable at the height of the Industrial Revolution, but like the entrepreneurial structure it is no longer so.

The third kind of configuration or design, the *professional organization*, is pulled by its *operating core* towards professionalized autonomy. That is, it is dominated by highly trained professional specialists. These have to be employed because the work is too complex to be controlled and coordinated in any other way. So it is broken up into specialisms, and people are hired to do it who already have standardized skills. That means professionals already trained and indoctrinated who can be relied on to do what has to be done. This is the situation in universities, hospitals, schools, accountancy firms, social work agencies, and some firms that employ highly skilled craftspeople (e.g. in fashion textiles designing). Since others without the training cannot interfere, the professionals are relatively independent. Their working autonomy is usually reinforced by a high demand for the service they give. Hence whilst the machine organization is run by hierarchical authority, the professional organization emphasizes the power of expertise. While the machine organization sets its own standards, the bureaucratic administrative framework of a professional organization accepts standards set externally by professional bodies such as the medical and accounting institutions.

This design of organization is uniquely democratic, but it suffers from difficulties of coordination and jurisdiction. Who should teach the statistics course in the management degree, the staff of the mathematics department or the business department? And who can declare a professor incompetent, and what then can be done about it?

The *diversified organization* is most widely used by large private industrial corporations, but it can also be seen in those American universities that have several campuses, or in health administrations which control several hospitals, and generally in socialist economies where government ministries control numbers of enterprises. It piggybacks on the machine organization, for it is a headquarters controlling several of them. These make a powerful *middle line*, in Mintzberg's terminology, the key part around which the organization functions. It is pulled towards Balkanization, for each division is relatively self-sufficient with its own marketing, purchasing and manufacturing (or equivalent) and so on, and each operates in its own market. Indeed, the diversified form is usually the result of a machine organization diversifying across more than one market, either into different products or into different geographical areas.

Though each division has a great deal of autonomy, headquarters decides how much capital each shall have and watches numerical performance indicators such as profits, sales and return on investment. This is where the problems arise. Headquarters may meddle too much in divisional decisions, and its concentration on numerical indicators may neglect other considerations such as product quality or environmental preservation. Mintzberg suspects that though the diversified organization is a fashionable sign of the times, it may be the most vulnerable of the five designs to legal and social changes.

In contrast, a space agency, an avant-garde film company, a factory making complex prototypes, or a petrochemicals company, is likely to be designed as an *innovative organization* or *adhocracy*. These are young research-based organizations which need to innovate in rapidly changing conditions. The primary key part of an adhocracy is the *support staff* in research and development, but there may also be key operating core personnel, experts on whom innovation depends. Unlike the professional organization, the adhocracy is not seeking the repetitive use of professionally standardized skills. Instead, it groups its highly trained specialists in mixed project teams, hoping to generate new ideas. It is pulled towards coordination within and between teams by 'mutual adjustment' (see Thompson, p. 66), i.e. by direct cooperation. Unified bureaucratic controls might get in the way. Of the five designs of organization, 'Adhocracy shows the least reverence for the classical principles of management' (e.g. as promulgated by Fayol, p. 97). It is uniquely both organic and decentralized.

There are two variants of adhocracy. An operating adhocracy works directly for clients, as in an advertising agency, whereas an administrative adhocracy serves itself, as did the National Aeronautics and Space Agency, NASA, in building up American space exploration.

Inevitably, adhocracy creates difficulties as well as innovations. People talk a lot, and this costs time. There is confusion over who is doing what. It is the most politicized design, breeding internal competition and conflict. But its strength in enabling flexibility of response means that new industries rely on this configuration. Mintzberg maintains that adhocracy is the structure of our present age, and he also confesses that this is the type of organization that he likes best.

The *missionary organization* does not have a key part, as such. Its key glue, which holds everything together, is the possession of an ideology, i.e. a rich system of distinctive values and beliefs shared by all the members. It is rooted in a deep sense of mission, associated with charismatic leadership and developed through strongly held traditions which reinforce the identification of the individual with the organization. Coordination is through standardization of norms, reinforced by selection and indoctrination of members. In the West, we had thought this approach to be appropriate to religious institutions, but Japanese corporations have shown that it can be successfully applied in business settings. And not only in Japanese culture. Many American firms have an overlay of the missionary approach, e.g. McDonald's or Hewlett-Packard, and build their effectiveness on an organizational ideology.

The final configuration is the *political organization*, which does not have overall coordinating mechanisms but is characterized by conflict. All organizations have a degree of conflict, where some 'political' activity takes place. This does not prejudice the organization's functioning, and indeed has a positive role to play in stimulating change. But when the conflict is pervasive, the organization has become politicized. This form characterizes some large public-sector institutions riven by conflicting approaches about both methods and objectives; and by private corporations after takeovers and mergers. If the conflict cannot be reduced, then the organization will not survive – unless it is artificially protected by, for example, the government.

It is important for managers to understand the configuration of their particular organization in order to ensure that the various parts 'fit together' and are consistent in what they do. But, Mintzberg warns, do not forget that there will always be contradictions among the forces in organizations. Managers should use these contradictions creatively, not ignore or try to suppress them.

BIBLIOGRAPHY

MINTZBERG, H., 'The Manager's Job: Folklore and Fact', *Harvard Business Review* (1975), 49–61; reprinted in D. S. Pugh (ed.), *Organization Theory*, Penguin, 1997.

MINTZBERG, H., *The Structuring of Organizations*, Prentice-Hall, 1979.

MINTZBERG, H., *The Nature of Managerial Work*, Harper & Row, 1973; Prentice-Hall, 1980.

MINTZBERG, H., *Mintzberg on Management*, Free Press, 1989.

Charles Handy

Charles Handy is a British writer and broadcaster. Born in Ireland, he has been an oil company executive, a business economist and a professor at the London Business School. He was Warden of St George's House in Windsor Castle, which is a centre for discussion of issues of business ethics, on which topic he takes a Christian approach. He has served as Chairman of the Royal Society for the Encouragement of Arts, Manufacture and Commerce, and was the 1994 British Business Columnist of the year. His concern is with the changing nature of work and organizations in modern economy and society.

Handy distinguishes four types of organizations, each symbolized by its characteristic Ancient Greek god. Each generates a distinctive organizational culture which pervades all its activities. The first type is the *club culture*, thought of as presided over by Zeus, who epitomizes the strong leader who has power and uses it. The visual image of this culture is a spider's web. Although there may be formal organizational departments and lines of authority, the only lines that matter are those, formal or informal, leading to the boss at the centre of the web. Most organizations begin in this culture, where the strength is in speed of decision. A limitation is that the quality of the decisions depends entirely on the calibre of the boss and the inner circle, since others can make little impact. You advance in this organization by learning to think and act as the boss would have done in your situation.

The second type of organization is the *role culture*, with its patron god Apollo, the god of order and rules. It is pictured as a Greek temple, where the pillars represent the functions and divisions of the organization. Within them it is assumed that people are rational, and that roles are defined, allocated and carried out according to systems of rules and procedures. It is the culture that Weber (p. 7) called bureaucratic and Burns (p. 53) mechanistic, and many large organizations which value stability and predictability are of this type: government administration, insurance corporations, organizations with a long history of success with one product or service, for example. Its strength is shown when tomorrow can be expected to be like yesterday; conversely its weakness is its slowness to recognize the need for strategic change and its inability to adapt.

The third type is the *task culture* of Athena, goddess of knowledge. In this culture management is regarded as a series of problems to be solved. First define the problem, then allocate resources for its solution, including people, machines and money. The picture of the organization is a net because it draws resources from all parts of the system. It is a network of loosely linked matrix structures in which task forces, working parties, *ad hoc* groups, etc., are brought together to achieve a particular goal. It is the culture that Burns (p. 53) called organic (or organismic). It works well when flexibility is required because the organization's output is a series of solutions to particular problems, e.g., in consultancy companies, advertising agencies, R & D departments. But these cultures do not function well when repetition and predictability are required, or when low costs are a major factor in success.

The final type of organization is the *existential culture* presided over by Dionysus, god of wine and song. The key difference here is that, unlike the other types, where the individual is subordinate to the aims of the organization, in this type the organization exists to help in the achievement of the individual's aims. For example, groups of professionals such as doctors, lawyers or architects can come together to create an organization in order to share an office, a telephone, a secretary. In these organizations the individual professionals are supreme; they recognize no 'boss', although they may accept coordination from a committee of their peers. These organizations are so democratic that there are few sanctions available to administrators. Management, which is regarded as a chore, requires general consent which leads to endless negotiation to obtain any coordinated effort.

There are no business or industrial organizations which operate completely with this last culture. But we are now witnessing an important change in the nature of organizations; in that they find it efficient to contract out more and more of their work to independent professionals. Organizations will therefore have to deal more and more with those who take a Dionysian view of the world.

This is only one of a number of changes that we are currently experiencing in regard to employment. They are not part of a predictable pattern, but are *discontinuous* changes in society. Such discontinuities happen from time to time in history. The change in the basis of economic activity from agriculture to industry was a previous example of this. The change now is from profitability based on machine power and brawn to profitability based on intelligence and professional skills. McKinsey, the management consultants, have estimated that by the year 2000, 80 per cent of all jobs will require cerebral rather than manual skills, a complete reversal from fifty years earlier.

In this new situation, both the nature of work and the nature of organizations are changing. In general, people can no longer expect to work for the whole of their lives in one occupation, perhaps for one employer. Organizations can no longer afford the overheads of carrying large numbers of people who may only be wanted for part of the time. Instead, work must be re-conceptualized in a much more flexible way as a 'portfolio of activities' based on professional knowledge and skill which an individual is able to offer to a number of organizations.

Handy uses the Irish national emblem, the shamrock, to characterize the ways in which people are linked to modern organizations. The *shamrock organization* has three parts to it: comparable to the three leaves which the clover-like shamrock has on each stem. Each part represents a different category of contribution to the organization by separate groups of people who have differing expectations and who are managed and paid differently.

The first group is the *professional core* of qualified professionals, technicians and managers. They are people who are essential to the organization, owning the organizational knowledge which distinguishes it from its competitors. They are therefore hard to replace, and the organization pays them high salaries and offers fringe benefits. In return the organization wants commitment, hard work and long hours. They are managed in the task culture and are thus expected to be flexibly available to go anywhere at any time and do what is required. For this they are paid more and more. This means that they are expensive, and organizations look for ways to reduce their numbers. Downsizing has been characteristic of organizations in recent years but output has gone up: half the number, paid twice as much, producing three times the output, appears to be the aim.

With a smaller core, more and more work is contracted out to specialists who can do it more efficiently and cheaply. So a *contractual fringe* has come into being and is taking a larger and larger proportion of the work. This is the second part of the shamrock. Manufacturing firms typically make fewer and fewer of the components of their products. They have become assemblers of parts manufactured by suppliers, hence the importance of Japanese just-in-time delivery systems. Organizations regularly contract out activities that were once regarded as a normal part of their work: advertising and market research, computing, catering, etc. The contractual fringe is made up of individuals and organizations who are paid for the results achieved, i.e. fees not wages, and this has great importance for the way in which they are managed. They are paid for output achieved, not for hours spent at work. But organizations are much more used to paying employees for time, and have to learn to manage the contractual relationship effectively across a very wide range of activities.

The third part of the organization is the *flexible labour force*. These are the part-time and temporary workers who are the fastest growing part of the employment market. As organizations wish both to increase their ability to respond to variations in demand and to improve profitability, they turn to this force to give them additional flexibility. Since people in this force are part-time or seasonal employees, there is a problem that employers may regard this part of the organization as merely casual labour. But if these workers are treated casually, they will be casual in their attitudes to the organization and its outputs, which means that the standards aimed for will not be reached. They are managed in the role culture, and although they will never have the commitment of the core, they have to be treated fairly if they are to be adequate in their roles.

Along with the development of the shamrock organization has come another discontinuous change in the nature of authority in organizations; namely the emergence of the *federal organization*. This is more than just a decentralized organization, for the logic of that form implies that knowledge and power are at the top of the hierarchy and certain amounts of them are handed down to the component parts. In the federal organization the logic goes the other way, with the subsidiaries federating together to get benefits of scale, but where the drive and energy come mostly from the parts. The centre is small; it does not direct or control the activities of the parts, rather it advises and influences, only reserving to itself a few key decisions e.g. capital allocations, appointment of top executives. Its vital task is to give a vision which shapes and gives a point to the work of all the parts. Handy compares this form of organization to a university or college, where the top management group can have only limited understanding about the large range of teaching and research activities being carried out.

For federalism to work well, two key principles must be understood and practised. The first is *subsidiarity*: the principle that the larger and higher body should not exercise functions which can be carried out efficiently by smaller and lesser bodies. For those at the centre, this is a much more difficult concept to put into practice than it appears, because a considerable amount of trust and confidence is required. The centre cannot be sure if the subsidiary organization can carry out the function efficiently before it has actually done so. But, in a catch-22 situation, if it uses this lack of experience as an argument against allowing them to try, then subsidiarity will never occur.

The second principle refers to those in the subsidiaries: they must want to increase the range of activities in their roles. Handy uses the analogy of the *inverted doughnut* to focus on the changing nature of organizational roles. A doughnut (or bagel) has a hole in the middle; the inverted doughnut is filled in the middle but the surround is empty up to the round contours of the edge. The core represents that part of the job which is fully prescribed, often in a job description, which, if not done well, will be seen as a clear failure on the part of the job occupant. But there will also be discretionary opportunities in a job, which no one has specified but which, if carried out effectively, will be regarded as showing appropriate initiative. These can fill the space up to the outside rim of the doughnut, which represents the boundaries of the discretion allowed in the job.

Traditionally, jobs in organizations have had large cores and small areas of discretion, as in an Apollo role culture. This allows control of the processes and of the behaviour of the people. In federal organizations, there are much smaller cores, since the exercise of discretion by subsidiary staff is key for subsidiarity to occur. These are more likely to be the task cultures of Athena. Controls can only be exercised after the event through 'management by results', and mistakes will inevitably occur. Managements have to learn to forgive mistakes and not always punish them, because this is how learning takes place.

BIBLIOGRAPHY

HANDY, C., *The Gods of Management*, Souvenir Press, 1978; Pan Books, 1979.

HANDY, C., *Understanding Organizations*, 3rd edn, Penguin, 1985.

HANDY, C., *The Age of Unreason*, Business Books, 1989.

HANDY, C., *The Empty Raincoat*, Hutchinson, 1994 (published in the US as *The Age of Paradox*, Harvard Business School Press).

HANDY, C., *Beyond Certainty*, Hutchinson, 1995.

HANDY, C., 'Trust and the Virtual Organization' in *Harvard Business Review* (May–June 1995), 40–50; reprinted in D. S. Pugh (ed.), *Organization Theory*, Penguin, 1997.

Christopher Bartlett and Sumantra Ghoshal

Christopher Bartlett and Sumantra Ghoshal are business school academics who have studied the functioning of corporations which operate internationally. Bartlett is a professor at the Harvard Business School; Ghoshal is at the London Business School. Their research leads them to propose that a new type of organizational structure, with its concomitant distinctive managerial thinking, is required for success in the current global business environment.

Bartlett and Ghoshal maintain that the world's largest companies are in flux, as global pressures have forced them to rethink their traditional worldwide strategies. While some firms have prospered, most are struggling for survival. Even within particular industries big differences have been manifested in performance. For example, within the consumer electronics industry the Japanese Matsushita corporation has prospered, whereas the American General Electric was eventually forced to sell off its business in this sector. It is not just a matter of the Japanese being better at it than the Americans. In the soap and detergent market the American Proctor & Gamble was able to mount a major thrust into international markets, whereas the international efforts of Kao, the dominant Japanese competitor in this industry, have stalled.

The key is the organization's capability for effective international operations. This is a combination of its strategic posture, its organization structure and its attitude to learning and innovation. For each firm the particular characteristics of its organizational capability have been built up over previous decades in response to the problems faced. This administrative heritage is an organizational asset, but it has to be examined very carefully and questioned, since it is also a constraint in adapting to new global environmental demands.

In the 1980s three distinct types of cross-national firms, each with different capabilities, could be identified:

Multinational companies
Global companies
International companies

Multinational companies have developed a strategic posture and structure which allows them to be very sensitive to differences in national environments. Their key capability is *responsiveness*. They build a strong local presence by responding to local market opportunities and are prepared to vary their products and even their businesses as necessary in the different countries. Firms such as the Anglo-Dutch Unilever and the American ITT were pioneers in developing links to each host country's infrastructure and thus creating conglomerates. These are relatively decentralized confederations with distributed resources and responsibilities. The control exercised may be limited to little more than the supervision of financial results.

Global companies are those which are driven by the need for common global operations, and are thus much more centralized in their strategic and operational decisions. Their key capability is *efficiency*. They obtain cost advantages through building world-scale facilities to distribute standard products to markets everywhere. It is a form pioneered in the motor industry by Ford, and is the approach taken by many Japanese companies such as Matsushita and Toyota. The centre retains strong control in decision-making, and foreign operations are seen as delivery mechanisms to global markets. Products and strategies are developed to exploit what is regarded as a worldwide unitary market.

International companies base their strategy primarily on transferring and adapting the parent company's knowledge and expertise to foreign markets. Their key capability is *transfer of learning*. The parent company retains considerable influence, but local units can adapt products and ideas coming from the centre. Firms such as the American IBM and the Swedish Ericsson run a 'coordinated federation' in which the subsidiaries have more autonomy than in the global company but less than in the multinational firm. Particular functions such as R & D, product and market development and finance are kept close to the centre. So there is a degree of benefit in both responsiveness to local markets and integrated global development.

Within the last decade, because of the turbulence of the global environment, none of these three types of structure and its accompanying capability has been adequate for success. For example, customers are demanding differentiated products as provided by the multinational company, but with the same high quality and low costs as standard products provided by the global company. There are also frequent changes in economic, technological, political and social environments which require the firm to be readily responsive. But, in addition, the organization has to build in the capability to continue to be responsive to the inevitable changes that occur in tastes, technologies, exchange rates, etc.

A new form of organization has been emerging to cope with this complex and changing global situation. It does not demand responsiveness *or* efficiency *or* learning as the key capability, but requires all three to be achieved simultaneously. This is the *transnational* form of organization, in which managers accept that each of the three previous types is partially true and has its own merits, but none represents the whole truth. Bartlett and Ghoshal put forward the transnational organization concept as a managerially sophisticated ideal type towards which cross-national organizations will have to develop in order to obtain and retain global competitiveness.

In the transnational company there is developed an *integrated network* structure in which neither centralization nor decentralization is embraced as a principle, but selective decisions about location and authority have to be made. Certain activities may be best centralized within the home country (e.g. basic research, treasury function) but others are best concentrated in certain subsidiaries (e.g. component production in low-wage economies, technical development in countries with a technically sophisticated infrastructure) while yet others are decentralized to many national operations (e.g. differentiated product assembly, sales). So, for example, an American transnational may obtain the benefits of world-scale production for labour-intensive products by building in a low-wage economy like Mexico, while obtaining the benefits of producing technically sophisticated products in Germany, and assembling both in Britain for the European market. Thus there is a considerable degree of functional and national specialization, which requires the interdependencies to be well managed. Frequently these interdependencies are designed to build self-enforcing cooperation among different units, such as when the French subsidiary depends on Spain for one range of products, while the Spanish one depends on France for another.

The transnational organization requires a distinctively different approach from previous forms of international operations. Its management has the key task of developing a set of strategic capabilities and relevant organizational characteristics as shown in the table.

Building and Managing the Transnational		
Strategic Capability	Organizational Characteristics	Management Tasks
Global competitiveness	Dispersed and interdependent assets and resources	Legitimizing diverse perspectives and capabilities
Multinational flexibility	Differentiated and specialized subsidiary roles	Developing multiple and flexible coordination processes
Worldwide learning	Joint development and worldwide sharing of knowledge	Building shared vision and individual commitment

from Bartlett and Ghoshal (1989)

To obtain global competitiveness with the transnational's dispersed and interdependent assets and resources requires balancing diverse capabilities and perspectives. As Crozier (p. 149) and Hickson (p. 16) have shown, the group that copes with the most critical strategic tasks of the organization gains power. So, for example, in Unilever (a 'multinational' company), it was the geographic managers who became dominant, because their contribution was crucial to achieving the dispersed responsiveness required. But in Matsushita (a 'global' company) it was the product division-managers who dominated, since they were the key to the company's world-scale efficiency. In IBM (an 'international' company) the strong technical and marketing groups retained their power through all reorganizations, since they were the basis of the company's strategy of building and transferring its core competencies for worldwide learning. The transnational company, however, must develop a multidimensional organization structure that legitimizes diversity and eliminates any bias that favours the management of any particular function, product or geographical area.

Similarly, the transnational needs to develop flexible coordination processes among the highly specialized and differentiated roles of its subsidiaries. It cannot rely on one preferred way of obtaining control. The preferred American way of a formalized control system (e.g. as in ITT), the preferred Japanese way of a centralized decision-making structure (e.g. as in Kao), the preferred European way of a socialization process for instilling a common culture (e.g. as in Unilever) are all inadequate by themselves for the transnational. This requires a portfolio of highly flexible coordination processes calling on all these approaches. These are used in appropriate ways for different types of national subsidiaries.

One type of national subsidiary may act as a *strategic leader* in a particular product market. For example, the Phillips subsidiary in the UK is the lead company for the whole corporation in the teletext market. The dominant approach to coordination in this case is the process of socialization. Another type of subsidiary may act in a *contributor* role. This type has a good local-resource capability but is operating in a market of limited strategic importance. An example is Ericsson's Australian subsidiary, which made important contributions to the development of its telephone-switching business, but whose home market is limited. It therefore has to be developed to contribute more widely to international operations. In this case direct headquarters coordination is appropriate. A further type of national subsidiary is the *implementer*, which carries out the corporation's operations in a market of limited potential. For example, Proctor and Gamble created teams to develop Euro Brands which could be marketed on a coordinated European basis. This required its subsidiaries in various European countries to refrain from modifying the formula, changing the packaging or adjusting the advertising approach in order for the company to obtain efficiencies of scale. This implementer type of subsidiary is coordinated by formalized systems, which require the least corporate-management time.

The internal differentiation both of subsidiary company roles and types of coordination processes – which may change from issue to issue – can lead to severe conflict in a transnational. The need for worldwide sharing of knowledge can cause difficulties too. Therefore a final key task of the central management is the need to unify the organization through a shared corporate vision. This requires clarity, continuity and consistency of purpose. Transnational organizations have to work to establish and communicate these attributes if they are to form the basis for the generation of individual commitment. It requires, among other things, a sophisticated

Human Resource Management system, which pays particular attention to training and development and to career management in an international setting.

Bartlett and Ghoshal are very clear that the complex transnational structure is not just a more sophisticated matrix structure. It is much more than that, since a new management mind-set is needed to understand the multidimensional nature of the tasks and to be prepared to interact openly and flexibly with others on them. As they put it: 'The task is not to build a sophisticated matrix structure, but to create a "matrix in the minds of managers".'

BIBLIOGRAPHY

BARTLETT, CHRISTOPHER A., and GHOSHAL, SUMANTRA, 'Managing across Borders: New Organizational Responses', *Sloan Management Review*, 1987 (Fall), 43–53; reprinted in D. S. Pugh (ed.), *Organization Theory*, Penguin, 1997.

BARTLETT, CHRISTOPHER A., and GHOSHAL, SUMANTRA, *Managing across Borders: The Transnational Solution*, Century Business, 1989.

TWO

The Organization in Its Environment

The beginning of administrative wisdom is the awareness that there is no one optimum type of management system.
TOM BURNS

The effective organization has integrating devices consistent with the diversity of its environment. The more diverse the environment and the more differentiated the organization, the more elaborate the integrating devices.
PAUL LAWRENCE and JAY LORSCH

Uncertainties pose major challenges to rationality.
JAMES D. THOMPSON

The key to organizational survival is the ability to acquire and maintain resources.
JEFFREY PFEFFER and GERALD R. SALANCIK

Efficient organizations establish mechanisms that complement their market strategy.
RAYMOND E. MILES and CHARLES C. SNOW

An ecology of organizations seeks to understand how social conditions affect the rates at which new organizations and new organizational forms arise, the rates at which organizations change forms, and the rates at which organizations and forms die out.
MICHAEL T. HANNAN and JOHN FREEMAN

Whether they like it or not the headquarters of multinationals are in the business of multicultural management.
GEERT HOFSTEDE

All organizations are situated in an environment, be that, for example, business, governmental, educational or voluntary service. In this environment are other organizations and people with whom transactions have to take place. These will include suppliers, clients or customers, and competitors. In addition there will be more general aspects of the environment which will have important effects, such as legal, technological and ethical developments.

The writers in this section have been concerned to analyse how the need to function successfully in different environments has led organizations to adopt different structures and strategies. Tom Burns examines the effects of rapidly changing technological developments on the attempts of old-fashioned firms to adjust to new environments. Paul Lawrence and Jay Lorsch emphasize that it is the appropriateness of the organization's structure in relation to its environmental requirements which is the basis of effectiveness.

James D. Thompson portrays organizations as open systems having to achieve their goals in the face of uncertainty in their environments. Jeffrey Pfeffer and Gerald Salancik argue for a 'resource dependence perspective' which sees all organizational functioning as resulting from the organization's interdependence with its environment. Raymond Miles and Charles Snow emphasize the strategic choices that managements have to make to adapt to the environmental pressures they face, while Michael Hannan and John Freeman take an ecological and evolutionary view of the chances of organizations surviving in their particular environments.

Geert Hofstede highlights national culture as it affects management values and processes. This environmental feature is particularly important in the ever more frequent international activities of organizations.

Tom Burns

Tom Burns spent more than thirty years at the University of Edinburgh, retiring in 1981 as Professor of Sociology. His early interests were in urban sociology, and he worked with the West Midland Group on Post-War Reconstruction and Planning. While he was at Edinburgh his particular concern was with studies of different types of organization and their effects on communication patterns and on the activities of managers. He has also explored the relevance of different forms of organization to changing conditions – especially to the impact of technical innovation.

In collaboration with a psychologist (G. M. Stalker), Burns has studied the attempt to introduce electronics development work into traditional Scottish firms, with a view to their entering this modern and rapidly expanding industry as the markets for their own well-established products diminished. The difficulties which these firms faced in adjusting to the new situation of continuously changing technology and markets led him to describe two 'ideal types' of management organization which are the extreme points of a continuum along which most organizations can be placed.

The *mechanistic* type of organization is adapted to relatively stable conditions. In it the problems and tasks of management are broken down into specialisms within which each individual carries out an assigned, precisely defined, task. There is a clear hierarchy of control, and the responsibility for overall knowledge and coordination rests exclusively at the top of the hierarchy. Vertical communication and interaction (i.e. between superiors and subordinates) is emphasized, and there is an insistence on loyalty to the concern and obedience to superiors. This system corresponds quite closely to Weber's rational–legal bureaucracy (see p. 7).

The *organismic* (also called *organic*) type of organization is adapted to unstable conditions when new and unfamiliar problems continually arise, which cannot be broken down and distributed among the existing specialist roles. There is therefore a continual adjustment and redefinition of individual tasks, and the contributive rather than restrictive nature of specialist knowledge is emphasized. Interactions and communication (information and advice rather than orders) may occur at any level as required by the process, and a much higher degree of commitment to the aims of the organization as a whole is generated. In this system, organization charts laying down the exact functions and responsibilities of each individual are not found, and indeed their use may be explicitly rejected as hampering the efficient functioning of the organization.

The almost complete failure of the traditional Scottish firms to absorb electronics research and development engineers into their organizations leads Burns to doubt whether a mechanistic firm can consciously change to an organismic one. This is because individuals in a mechanistic organization are not only committed to the organization as a whole, but are also members of a group or department with a stable career structure and with sectional interests in conflict with those of other groups. Thus there develop power struggles between established sections to obtain control of the new functions and resources. These divert the organization from purposive adaptation and allow out-of-date mechanistic structures to be perpetuated and 'pathological' systems to develop.

Pathological systems are attempts by mechanistic organizations to cope with new problems of change, innovation and uncertainty while sticking to the formal bureaucratic structure. Burns describes three of these typical reactions. In a mechanistic organization the normal procedure for dealing with a matter outside an individual's sphere of responsibility is to refer it to the appropriate specialist or, failing that, to a superior. In a rapidly changing situation the need for such consultations occurs frequently; and in many instances the superior has to put up the matter higher still. A heavy load of such decisions finds its way to the chief executive, and it soon becomes apparent that many decisions can only be made by going to the top. Thus there develops the *ambiguous figure system* of an official hierarchy and a non-officially-recognized system of pair relationships between the Chief Executive and some dozens of people at different positions in the management structure. The head of the concern is overloaded with work, and many senior managers whose status depends on the functioning of the formal system feel frustrated at being bypassed.

Some firms attempted to cope with the problems of communication by creating more branches of the bureaucratic hierarchy, e.g. contract managers, liaison officers. This leads to a system described as the *mechanistic jungle*, in which a new job or even a whole new department may be created, whose existence depends on the perpetuation of these difficulties. The third type of pathological response is the *super-personal* or *committee system*. The committee is the traditional way of dealing with temporary problems which cannot be solved within a single individual's role without upsetting the balance of power. But as a permanent device it is inefficient, in that it has to compete with the loyalty demanded and career structure offered by the traditional departments. This system was tried only sporadically by the firms, since it was disliked as being typical of inefficient government administration; attempts to develop the committee as a super-person to fulfil a continuing function that no individual could carry out met with little success.

For a proper understanding of organizational functioning, Burns maintains, it is therefore always necessary to conceive of organizations as the simultaneous working of at least three social systems. The first of these is the formal authority system derived from the aims of the organization, its technology, its attempts to cope with its environment. This is the overt system in terms of which all discussion about decision-making takes place. But organizations are also cooperative systems of people who have career aspirations and a career structure, and who compete for advancement. Thus decisions taken in the overt structure inevitably affect the differential career prospects of the members, who will therefore evaluate them in terms of the career system as well as the formal system, and will react accordingly. This leads to the third system of relationships which is part of an organization – its political system. Every organization is the scene of 'political' activity in which individuals and departments compete and cooperate for power. Again all decisions in the overt system are evaluated for their relative impact on the power structure as well as for their contribution to the achievement of the organization's goals.

It is naive to consider the organization as a unitary system equated with the formal system, and any change to be successful must be acceptable in terms of the career structure and the political structure as well. This is particularly so with modern, technologically based organizations which contain qualified experts who have a career structure and a technical authority which goes far beyond the organization itself and its top management. Thus the attempt to change from a mechanistic to an organismic management structure has enormous implications for the career structure (which is much less dependent on the particular organization) and the power system (which is much more diffuse, deriving from technical knowledge as much as formal position).

Concern with the interaction of these three social systems within the organization continues in Burns's study of the British Broadcasting Corporation. The BBC is a very segmented organization both horizontally, where there are a large number of departments (e.g. Drama, Outside Broadcasts, Finance) which appear to be competing as much as cooperating, and vertically, where in order to rise in the grading structure executives soon lose contact with the professional skills (e.g. journalism, engineering) which they are supposed to administer. In this situation the career and the political systems can become more important than the formal task system.

Burns charts the rise in power of the central management of the BBC at the expense of the creative and professional staff, which stems from the Corporation's financial pressures. He maintains that the Corporation can only develop as a creative service dedicated to the public good if it is freed from its financial-client relationship to the government.

'A sense of the past and the very recent past is essential to anyone who is trying to perceive the here-and-now of industrial organization.' If the organizational structure is viewed as a result of a process of continuous development of the three social systems of formal organization, career structure and political system, a study of this process will help organizations to avoid traps they would otherwise fall into. Adaptation to new and changing situations is not automatic. Indeed many factors militate against it. An important one is the existence of an organization structure appropriate to an earlier phase of development. Another is the multifaceted nature of the commitments of organizational members: to their careers, their departments, their specialist sub-units. These are often stronger than their commitment to the organization as a whole.

BIBLIOGRAPHY

BURNS, T., 'Industry in a New Age', *New Society*, 31 January 1963, no. 18; reprinted in D. S. PUGH (ed.), *Organization Theory*, Penguin, 1997.

BURNS, T., 'On the Plurality of Social Systems' in J. R. LAWRENCE (ed.), *Operational Research and the Social Sciences*, Tavistock, 1966.
BURNS, T., *The BBC: Public Institution and Private World*, Macmillan, 1977.
BURNS, T., and STALKER, G. M., *The Management of Innovation*, Tavistock, 1961; 3rd edn, Oxford University Press, 1994.

Paul Lawrence and Jay Lorsch

Paul Lawrence and Jay Lorsch were professorial colleagues in Organizational Behaviour at the Harvard Business School. Together with many collaborators (who include S. A. Allan, S. M. Davis, J. Kotter, H. Lane, and J. J. Morse), they have conducted a series of studies into the appropriate structure and functioning of organizations, using what has become known as the 'organization and environment' approach, described in their seminal book of that title.

Lawrence and Lorsch begin their analysis with the question of why people seek to build organizations. Their answer is that organizations enable people to find better solutions to the environmental problems facing them. This immediately highlights three key elements in their approach to understanding organizational behaviour: (i) it is people who have purposes, not organizations; (ii) people have to come together to coordinate their different activities into an organization; and (iii) the effectiveness of the organization is judged by the adequacy with which the members' needs are satisfied through planned transactions with the environment.

It is in order to cope effectively with their external environments that organizations must come to develop segmented units, each of which has as its major task the problem of dealing with some aspect of the conditions outside the firm. For example, in a manufacturing firm with production, sales and design units, the production unit deals with production equipment sources, raw materials sources and labour markets; the sales unit faces problems with the market, the customers and the competitors; the design unit has to cope with technological developments, government regulations and so on. This *differentiation* of function and task is accompanied by differences in cognitive and emotional orientation among the managers in different units, and differences too, in the formal structure of different departments. For instance, the development department may have a long-term horizon and a very informal structure, whereas production may be dealing with day-to-day problems in a rigidly formal system, with sales facing the medium-term effects of competitors' advertising with moderate formality.

In spite of this the organization is a system which has to be coordinated so that a state of collaboration exists in order to reap the benefits of effective transactions with the environment. This is the required *integration* and it, too, is affected by the nature of the external conditions.

The basic necessity for *both* appropriate differentiation *and* adequate integration to perform effectively in the external environment is at the core of Lawrence and Lorsch's model of organizational functioning. The approach was developed in an important study which they carried out on ten firms in three different industries – plastics (six firms), food (two firms) and containers (two firms) which constituted very different environments for the enterprises concerned.

The study recognized that all the firms involved segment their environment. Each of the ten was dealing with a market sub-environment (the task of the sales department), a techno-economic sub-environment (the task of the manufacturing unit) and a scientific sub-environment (the task of the R & D or design department). The greater the degree of uncertainty within each sub environment and the greater the diversity between them, the greater was the need of the firms to *differentiate* between their sub-units of sales, production and research in order to be effective in each sub-environment. For example, in the plastics industry, which was found to have great diversity, with the science sub-environment highly uncertain but the techno-economic one relatively stable, a considerable degree of differentiation within effective firms was found. In the container industry, on the other hand, all parts of the environment were relatively certain and so a much lower degree of differentiation was apparent.

But greater differentiation brings with it potential for greater inter-departmental conflict as the specialist groups develop their own ways of dealing with the particular uncertainties of their own sub-environments. These differences are not just minor variations in outlook but may involve fundamental ways of thinking and behaving. In the plastics industry a sales manager may be discussing a potential new product in terms of whether it will perform in the customers' machinery, whether they will pay the cost and whether it can be got on to the market in three months' time. The research scientist at the same meeting may be thinking about whether the molecular structure of the material could be changed without affecting its stability and whether doing this would open out a line of research for the next two years which would be more interesting than other projects. These two specialists not only think differently, they dress differently, they have different habits of punctuality, and so on. It therefore becomes crucial that a highly differentiated firm should have appropriate methods of *integration* and conflict resolution if they are to perform well in the environment.

The table opposite lists the integrative devices which were found to be operating in three high-performing organizations, one from each of the industries studied. The top row gives the rating for the degree of differentiation, and it will be seen that the need to operate effectively in the plastics environment led the firm to develop a high degree of differentiation; the container firm had the lowest differentiation and the food firm was in between.

Each of these firms used a different combination of devices for achieving integration. All of them used to some extent the traditional methods of paper systems, the formal managerial hierarchy and direct managerial contact between members of the different departments. For the container firm with the least differentiation these methods were sufficient, but in the food firm, which had a greater need for integration, temporary teams made up of specialists from the units involved were set up to deal with any particularly urgent issue. Managers within functional departments were also assigned integrating roles such as that of liaison officer. Clearly the effective food firm was devoting a larger amount of time and effort to integrating activity.

The plastics organization had in addition established a special department, one of whose primary activities was integration. They also had an elaborate set of permanent integrating teams, each made up of members from the various functional units and the integrating department. The purpose of these teams was to provide a formal setting in which interdepartmental conflicts, such as the one described above between the sales manager and the research scientist, could be resolved with the help of an integrator. The effective plastics firm drew on the whole range of integrative devices and needed to do so because its necessary differentiation was so high.

It is the appropriateness of the three-way relationships between the uncertainty and diversity of the environment, the degree of organizational differentiation, and the state of integration and conflict resolution

Comparison of Integrative Devices in Three High-Performing Organizations

	Plastics	Food	Container
Degree of differentiation	10.7	8.0	5.7
Major integrative devices	(1) Integrative department	(1) Individual integrators	(1) Direct managerial contact
	(2) Permanent cross-functional teams at three levels of management	(2) Temporary cross-functional teams	(2) Managerial hierarchy
	(3) Direct managerial contact	(3) Direct managerial contact	(3) Paper system
	(4) Managerial hierarchy	(4) Managerial hierarchy	
	(5) Paper system	(5) Paper system	

from Lawrence and Lorsch (1967)

achieved, which will lead to effective functioning. Inadequacy in any of these relationships was associated with lower performance. Thus, for example, the high performers in the plastics and food industry had *both* greater differentiation *and* greater integration than the low performers, since both were required. By contrast, in the low-performing container organization there was no evidence that the integrating unit it possessed was serving a useful purpose given its low level of differentiation.

Effective conflict resolution, which is the behavioural basis of integration, was found to have a pattern in which inter-unit conflict is dealt with by managers working in a problem-solving mode to face the issues and work through to the best overall solution – rather than smoothing over the issues to avoid conflict, or letting the party with the greater power force its solution on others. It was also found that in dealing with conflict effectively, the individuals primarily involved in achieving integration (whether they be superiors in the line hierarchy, or persons appointed specifically to coordinating roles) need to have their authority based not just on their formal position, but largely on their knowledge of and competence on the issues as perceived by all the groups involved, together with a balanced orientation between the parties. The power and influence to make decisions leading to the resolution of conflict must therefore be located at the points where the knowledge to reach such decisions also exists.

The Lawrence and Lorsch framework, by emphasizing that the appropriate organization structure will depend upon the environmental demands, takes a 'contingency' approach, rejecting the formulation that one particular structural form (e.g. bureaucracy, see Weber, p. 7) or one particular motivational approach (e.g. Theory Y, see McGregor, p. 164) is always best. It is the appropriateness which is the key.

Lorsch and Morse, in a further study, compared two manufacturing plants (one high-performing, one low-performing) with two research laboratories (similarly high and low performers). The organization structures and processes of the high-performing manufacturer in a relatively certain environment were: high formality, short time-horizon, highly directive management. The individuals working in this organization were found to have low cognitive complexity, low tolerance for ambiguity and dependency in authority relationships. The high-performing research laboratory in a relatively uncertain environment had low formality, long time-horizons and high participation. Its members had high cognitive complexity, high tolerance for ambiguity and independence in authority relationships. Yet both organizations were effective because they were appropriately organized with appropriate members for their environmental tasks. Indeed the less effective organization in each pair did not show most of the distinctive characteristics of structure and process to the same degree. On the other hand the characteristics of the members were as clearly differentiated as in the successful organizations. These less effective organizations, it seems, could obtain the appropriate people but not organize them in the appropriate way. But equally, in other cases, failure could be due to having inappropriate people even though they were appropriately organized.

In a later study of seven major US industries, including those of steel, agriculture, hospitals and telecommunication, Lawrence and Dyer developed the 'competitive principle'. This maintains that an industry needs to experience an appropriate degree of vigorous competition in its environment if it is to be economically strong. Either too little or too much competition will lead to inefficient and non-innovative performance. They argue for the setting up of a government agency to monitor the competitive pressures in each industry to determine whether they need to be increased or reduced.

The analysis of matrix organizations has been a particular concern of Davis and Lawrence. Matrix organization structures are those in which there is a multiple command system – many managers having two bosses. For example, finance managers would have a finance director to whom they would be responsible for professional standards, and who would be concerned with their career development and promotion. In addition, each would also report to a project director to whom they would be responsible for giving the appropriate cost accounting services needed for their current project, and who would therefore be in charge of the day-to day work allocation. Clearly this form of structure violates Fayol's principle of 'unity of command' (see p. 99) and its greater complexity would be the preferred structure only in certain situations. These are when: (1) there are several highly salient sectors (i.e. products, markets, functions etc.) which are simultaneously necessary for goal achievement; (2) the tasks are uncertain, complex and interdependent; and (3) there is a need to realize economies by using scarce resources effectively. In these circumstances, there is a need for complex differentiation and integration via the matrix mode.

BIBLIOGRAPHY

LAWRENCE, P. R., and LORSCH, J. W., *Organization and Environment*, Harvard, 1967.

LAWRENCE, P. R., and LORSCH, J. W., *Developing Organizations: Diagnosis and Action,* Addison-Wesley, 1969.

LORSCH, J. W., and MORSE, J. J., *Organizations and Their Members: A Contingency Approach*, Harper & Row, 1974.

DAVIS, S. M., and LAWRENCE, P. R., *Matrix*, Addison-Wesley, 1977.

DONALDSON, G., and LORSCH, J. W., *Decision-Making at the Top*, Basic Books, 1983.

LAWRENCE, P. R., and DYER, D., *Renewing American Industry*, Free Press, 1983.

James D. Thompson

After leaving the American armed forces subsequent to the Second World War, James Thompson (1920–73) became a sociologist. Yet he made his contribution to the understanding of organizations through research in business schools. He was the founding editor of the world's leading research journal in organization theory, the *Administrative Science Quarterly*. He died prematurely only six years after the publication in 1967 of his classic book *Organizations in Action*. This book draws together a range of ideas which were forming at the time it was written, and which have continued to be at the centre of organization theory. It is a portrayal of complex organizations 'as open systems, hence indeterminate and faced with uncertainty, but at the same time as subject to criteria of rationality and hence needing determinateness and certainty'. It pictures organizations continually striving to act rationally in the face of technological and environmental uncertainties. Their basic problem is how to cope with these uncertainties.

In other words, organizations – or rather, their members – aspire to be reasoned and orderly despite circumstances and events which may prevent them being so. These standards, or *norms of rationality* to which they aspire, demand of organizations both coordination within, and adjustment without. The twin tasks of administration are to provide the needful coordination within the organization and the adjustment to circumstances outside it.

The first task therefore is to achieve the stable coordination of those basic work activities which Thompson calls the *technical core* of an organization. For example, in factory production work, supplies of components must be continuously in the right places at the right times if assembly is to proceed smoothly, just as in a college the teachers and students must be in the right rooms at the right times.

The second task of administration is to regulate transactions across the boundary of the organization, that is its contacts with the world outside itself. This might be done by negotiating with outside interests for, say, assured financial credit, or raw materials, or by changing with the environment, as when a chain of toy stores changes what it sells in response to rising public standards of safety for children. Or it might be done by *buffering*. Buffering protects the technical core from the uncertainties of acquiring resources, and of disposing of outputs (e.g. by having a purchasing department to handle suppliers and a sales department to deal with customers). A public relations department can cope with challenges to the rightfulness of what the organization is doing, as in the cases of nuclear power or cigarette manufacture. Such *boundary spanning units* are placed between the technical core and the outside world to buffer it from external shocks. Another possibility is to move the boundaries of the organization to encircle sources of uncertainty and bring them under control, for instance, to ensure supplies by buying up a supplier firm.

Hence organizations come to be made up of a variety of different parts. These can be linked together in fundamentally different ways, and so internal interdependence may differ from one organization to the next, and within any one organization. Interdependence can be pooled, sequential, or reciprocal. *Pooled interdependence* is where the work of each part of an organization is not directly connected to that of the others but is a 'discrete contribution to the whole'. Yet since each is supported by that whole organization, which in turn would be threatened by the failure of any of its parts, they have a pooled interdependence within it. Such is the situation in a university, where the departments of biology, French language, and management, for example, are not linked in any way other than by their common reliance upon the university as a whole.

In *sequential interdependence* one part cannot do its job until others have done theirs. Tasks have to be done in sequence, first this, then that. Such is the situation in a factory, where one workshop must machine components to the right sizes before the next can put them through a hardening treatment, and so on through successive stages up to the final product.

In *reciprocal interdependence* each does something for the other. Unlike the one-way flow in sequential interdependence, the output of each becomes input for the other. That is the situation in an airline, where the flight operations section constantly makes aircraft available to the maintenance engineers for servicing, and the engineers constantly turn out aircraft ready for the operations people to fly.

Reciprocal interdependence requires the closest coordination, sequential interdependence less, pooled interdependence least. While all organizations have a certain amount of pooled interdependence, and in some it may be the prevalent form, not all have sequential interdependence in addition to pooled, and fewer still have within them all these kinds of interdependence.

The various units are grouped in the hierarchy of an organization in such a way as to minimize the costs of coordinating what they do. The means of coordination differ. Reciprocally interdependent units have to coordinate what each does for the other by *mutual adjustment*, so they are likely to be placed together in the hierarchy under common superiors who can ensure that they cooperate. If units are sequentially interdependent, then their work can be coordinated by *planning or scheduling*, the work of each being planned to dovetail in sequence with that of the next in line. In a factory, a prior department in the sequence has to turn out enough components so that the next department in the sequence is not left standing idle. If there is merely pooled interdependence, then some coordination within the whole can be achieved by *standardization* of the rules which link each part with the whole: in a university, for example, though the departments differ in their contributions to the whole, in principle they are all to be dealt with in the same manner when it comes to examination procedures or budget allocations (which is not to say that they all get the same budget).

Organizations also differ in the activities undertaken by their technical core. They have one or more of three technologies. A *long-linked technology*, as in manufacturing, performs a series of tasks in a set order, giving rise to the sequential interdependence of units referred to earlier. A *mediating technology* links other parties, as where banks mediate between lenders and borrowers, or an employment agency mediates between prospective employers and employees. Thirdly, an *intensive technology* functions in response to feedback from the object worked upon, as where what is done and when it is done depend in a hospital upon the patient's condition, or at a construction site upon the condition of the ground.

The ways in which organizations attempt to encircle external sources of uncertainty by extending their boundaries are determined by these kinds of technology. Those with long-linked technologies tend to go for a corresponding vertical integration, as when oil refiners own roadside service stations and automobile manufacturers own suppliers of components.

Those with mediating technologies try to increase the populations they serve, so that airlines increase their route networks and banks put branches into new areas. Finally, organizations with intensive technology attempt to incorporate the object worked upon so as to control it better, for instance, universities making their students also their members and therefore subject to their rules, or mental hospitals bringing patients inside for observation.

This extension of boundaries is not the only way of coping with environmentally derived uncertainty. As also mentioned before, organizations can buffer their technical core by setting up boundary spanning units which allow the core to operate as if there were stability. By stockpiling supplies and outputs, for example, work can continue as if there were a steady stream of supplies and a steady demand by the market. Alternatively, fluctuations may be prevented, as when utilities offer cheap off-peak gas or electricity to smooth out demand, or may be anticipated, as when ice-cream production is adjusted to seasonal changes. If buffering, smoothing and anticipating fail, organizations can resort to rationing. So the post office gives priority to first-class mail, a hospital may deal only with urgent cases and a manufacturer may limit the proportion of popular items taken by any one wholesaler.

The relation between technical core and boundary spanning activities gives rise to appropriate types of structure. Where technical core and boundary spanning activities can be isolated from one another, there is likely to be in the hierarchy a layer of functionally specialized departments, such as purchasing and sales and finance, comparatively remote from the core and under central control. Where core and boundary activities are more closely interdependent, there is more likely to be a divisionalized structure, decentralized into 'self sufficient clusters' of units. Each cluster has only so much to deal with, for instance, as in a divisionalized multi-national firm which has one multi-department division covering Europe, another covering South East Asia, and so on.

Norms of rationality, which Thompson repeatedly stresses are assumed in all that he has to say about organizations, require that organizations 'keep score' so that their performances can be assessed. The problem is how to do this. Where it is possible to trace clearly the consequences of what is done (i.e. where there is a clear presumption that new equipment has reduced costs) then efficiency measures can be used. These assume understanding of cause and effect and known standards of performance, as is the case with many financial indicators in industry. However, if *intrinsic criteria* which indicate relatively directly the standard of work done are lacking, then *extrinsic criteria* have to be used. From these the quantity and quality of the work can be inferred, but they do not show it directly. Hence university research is measured by counting the money gained for it in competitive applications to funding institutions, and by the number of publications about it, rather than by its results as such, and mental hospitals emphasize discharge rates rather than the extent to which patients are cured.

Organizations are torn between the differing assessments made by a variety of assessors. The potential users of a public health service will look at it in one way; the government providing the money will look at it in another. The users are concerned with the treatment given; the government is concerned more with the cost of the treatment. Shareholders stress dividend and profits; customers stress prices. So each organization tries to do best on the criteria used by those on whom it is most dependent. Furthermore, it will try to score well on the most *visible criteria*. These are the most obvious to the most important assessors. Business firms are sensitive to the price of their stock on the stock exchange, schools announce the examination performances of top pupils, and so on. Less visible criteria may be neglected, even if they are intrinsically more desirable.

According to Thompson, the more sources of uncertainty there are, the more possibilities there are for gaining power (see also Crozier p. 149), and the more likely it is that 'political' positions will be taken up. In general, individuals higher in management have discretion in decisions and so what should be done is subject to their personal judgement, including their assessment of what will be acceptable to others. This political assessment would be crucial in deciding, for example, whether or not two departments could be successfully merged.

The making of decisions involves beliefs, or assumptions, as to what will happen if this is done rather than that, and preferences as to what is most desirable. There is less certainty about some beliefs and preferences than there is about others, as illustrated by Thompson's matrix:

Preferences regarding possible outcomes

		Certainty	Uncertainty
Beliefs about cause/effect relations	Certain	COMPUTATIONAL STRATEGY	COMPROMISE STRATEGY
	Uncertain	JUDGEMENTAL STRATEGY	INSPIRATIONAL STRATEGY

The matrix shows four likely kinds of *decision-making strategies*. The two left-hand boxes represent situations where there is relative certainty on what is wanted. Those concerned are clear on what outcome they prefer. In the top left-hand box they are also certain of what the consequences of their decision may be. Such all-round certainty might occur if they were considering increasing existing production capacity in response to a steady rise in sales. Agreed on the need to expand, and knowing the technology from past experience, management could confidently calculate likely costs and returns in a *computational* manner. However, the lower box represents a situation where cause and effect are less well known. Here the same management still wants to expand capacity but if they do they will have to buy new machinery of an untried design. This decision is less susceptible to computation, more a *judgemental* matter assessing the risk involved.

In the two right-hand boxes, managers are not sure what they want and there may be divided opinions. Alternative outcomes may each be attractive, for instance, increasing capacity either for mass production of low-quality products, or for a smaller volume of higher-quality products. If the technology for both is well known, and market forecasts are confident that either can be profitable, a *compromise* strategy results in some of each. However, if there is all-round uncertainty as in the lower right-hand box, then an *inspirational strategy* is more likely. There are neither clear preferences for high-volume against low-volume production, nor is there confidence in what the consequences of new production machinery or of launching more goods on to the market will be. The strategy has to be an inspired leap in the dark.

In Thompson's view, the aim of management and administration when designing organizations and making decisions must be the effective alignment of organization structure, technology and environment. This central conception has been and continues to be at the heart of organization theory, and it is a constant stimulus to research. Again and again his analysis is returned to as a source of ideas, few of which have been as yet supplanted.

BIBLIOGRAPHY

THOMPSON, J. D., *Organizations in Action*, McGraw-Hill, 1967.

Jeffrey Pfeffer and Gerald R. Salancik

Jeffrey Pfeffer and Gerald Salancik are respectively professors at the Stanford University Graduate School of Business, California, and Carnegie-Mellon University, Pittsburgh. Pfeffer and Salancik contend that organizations should be understood in terms of their interdependence with their environments. They advocate a *resource dependence perspective*. For example, explaining discontent among the employees of a fast-food chain by poor human relations and poor pay is irrelevant if the organization can draw on a pool of easily recruited youthful labour, and since its competitors can do so too, the organization is not going to incur the costs of better human relations and pay.

Organizations are not self-directed and autonomous. They need resources, including money, materials, personnel and information, and to get these they must interact with others who control the resources. This involves them in a constant struggle for autonomy as they confront external constraints. They become 'quasi-markets' in which influence is bartered not only between internal sections but between those sections or subunits and external interests.

Interdependence with others lies in the availability of resources and the demand for them. It is of many kinds. For instance, there is the direct dependence of a seller organization upon its customers, and there is the indirect dependence upon each other of two seller organizations, not in mutual contact, via a set of potential customers for whom they compete.

Three conditions define how dependent an organization is. First is the importance of a resource to it. This is a combination of the magnitude of that resource (in other words, the proportion of inputs and outputs accounted for by the resource), and of its criticality, best revealed by how severe the consequences would be if it were not available. Second is how much discretion those who control a resource have over its allocation and use. If they have completely free access to it and can make the rules about it, then an organization which needs it can be put in a highly dependent position. Third is how far those who control a resource have a monopoly of it. Can an organization which needs it find an alternative source or a substitute? Thus 'the potential for one organization's influencing another derives from its discretionary control over resources needed by that other, and the other's dependence on the resource and lack of countervailing resources or access to alternative sources.' Since the others on whom an organization depends may not be dependable, its effectiveness is indicated more by how well it balances these dependencies than by internal measures of efficiency of a financial or similar nature.

To Pfeffer and Salancik the possible strategies that an organization may use to balance its dependencies are of four kinds. It may:

1. Adapt to or alter constraints.
2. Alter the interdependencies by merger, diversification, or growth.
3. Negotiate its environment by interlocking directorships or joint ventures with other organizations or by other associations.
4. Change the legality or legitimacy of its environment by political action.

There are numerous ways of carrying out the first kind of strategy, adapting to or altering external constraints. An organization can pay sequential attention (see March, p. 139) to the demands made upon it, attending first to one and then to another as in turn they become more pressing. For example, for a time customers may take priority, then attention may switch to financial economies required by owners or lenders. An organization can play one interest off against another (e.g. blaming different unions for current difficulties). It can influence the formulation of demands (e.g. by advertising); it can claim that it cannot comply because of, say, legal restrictions; it can minimize its dependence by stocks of materials or money. And so on.

Merging, diversifying or growing are each ways of pursuing the second kind of strategy, altering the interdependent relationships. Mergers do this by bringing control of critical resources within one organization, stabilizing the exchanges of which they are part. They may be backwards, sideways or forwards, incorporating suppliers, competitors or purchasers. Diversification shifts and widens the interdependencies in which an organization is enmeshed, extricating it from over-dependence in any one field. Growth in size increases the power of an organization relative to others, and makes more people interested in its survival. Size has been found to improve stability more than profitability.

Third, negotiating the environment is a more common strategy than total absorption by merger. Interlocking directorships, whereby boards include members of the boards of other organizations, cartels to control supplies, trade agreements, memberships in trade associations and coordinating industry councils and advisory bodies, joint ventures in which two or more organizations work together, and the like, are commonplace. Such links help to keep the participating organizations informed about what is happening outside themselves and to ensure mutual commitment. Normative expectations build up as to what each other will do, making each more sure of the other's reliability.

Fourth, and finally, if none of the other strategies is open to them, organizations resort to political action. They endeavour to obtain and sustain favourable taxation, or tariffs, or subsidies, or licensing of themselves or their members (as where the practice of medicine or law, for example, is restricted to defined categories of qualified people), or they charge others with violating regulations (as when competitors are accused of prohibited monopolistic arrangements). There is constant political activity by organizations which give to political party funds, lobby the members of legislatures, and are represented on governmental and related agencies and councils. Indeed, if there is a high level of state regulation, the decisions of lawmakers and government agencies become more important to an organization than those of its customers or clients.

How are the effects of the environment, with whose elements an organization is interdependent, transmitted to that organization? It is generally accepted that environments affect organizations, but how that happens is not made explicit. Pfeffer and Salancik suggest that one means is executive succession. That is, the removal of executives and their replacement by others. Through this the environment influences the political processes within organizations from which action emerges.

There are three causal steps in Pfeffer and Salancik's argument about executive succession. To begin with, changes in whichever sectors of the environment are uncertain and which are less so mould the pattern of power in an organization. This occurs as posited by the 'strategic contingencies theory of intraorganizational power' formulated by Hickson, Hinings and their colleagues (see under Pugh and the Aston Group, p. 17). According to this theory, those sections or sub-units of organizations most able to cope with what is uncertain to an organization (e.g. a marketing department smoothing out erratic fluctuations in orders by shrewdly timed advertising, or a maintenance department keeping production flowing by skilled attention to breakdowns) gain power, subject to two conditions. They must be non-substitutable (no one else can do what they do) and central (many others in the organization are affected by what they do, and the organization's main outputs would be affected immediately if they ceased to do it).

The resulting distribution of power then affects the choice of top personnel. As Pfeffer and Salancik put it, 'We view administrative succession as a political process of contested capability, where the contest is resolved by sub-unit power.' There is a tendency to blame top management for difficulties, the counterpart to their own tendency to take credit for successes in a world over which they have limited control. So they tend to be removed if things go badly, and who is removed and who replaces them follows the perceptions the powerful of who can best cope with the perceived uncertain dependencies.

The third step in the argument is that executives and administrators once appointed can and do influence the main directive decisions. Although their control over their world is limited, they do have sufficient to shape decisions. They take part in what Child has called 'strategic choice' (see under Pugh and the Aston Group, p. 15), which delineates the intended future course of their organization. They 'enact' an environment, acting according to how they see it, and trying to change it to their organization's advantage. Further, changes in top personnel permit movement between organizations and this can be a tacit means of coordination. The managers of one know the managers in another.

Top managements are especially concerned with scanning the environment to find out what is happening and what may happen, and with loosening dependencies so that the organization does not become too dependent on any one or few others, and with managing conflicting external demands. It has been fashionable to forecast that the environment they face will become more and more dispersed and turbulent, but Pfeffer and Salancik do not agree. They foresee 'an increasingly interconnected environment in which power is increasingly concentrated'. Though they write in terms of the American variant of the capitalist system, their resource dependence perspective generalizes beyond that.

BIBLIOGRAPHY

PFEFFER, J., and SALANCIK, G. R., *The External Control of Organizations: A Resource Dependence Perspective*, Harper & Row, 1978.

Raymond E. Miles and Charles C. Snow

Raymond Miles and Charles Snow are both professors in American business schools. Miles is Professor of Business Administration at the University of California, Berkeley. He has studied and advised a wide variety of organizations in the public and private sectors. Snow is Professor of Organizational Behaviour at Pennsylvania State University.

Miles and Snow ask how and why organizations differ in strategy, in structure, in technology and in administration. Why do some offer a broad range of products or services and others a narrower range? Why are some structured around functional specialisms and others around product lines or services? Why are some more centralized, others more decentralized? For Miles and Snow the answers can be found with Thompson (see p. 64), in what he termed the alignment of organization with environment.

To align organization and environment successfully, management has to solve three problems, and solve them continuously. They are the entrepreneurial, engineering and administrative problems. The *entrepreneurial problem* is to choose a general market domain, or field of operation, in which the organization can be viable, to specify the precise target market and decide on the right products or services for it. Solving this problem, however, requires also solving the *engineering problem*, taking the word 'engineering' in a wide sense. Ways have to be found of making the products or offering the services. There must be appropriate technologies. Then the *administrative problem* is to organize and manage the work.

The aim should be an effective *adaptive cycle*. This means that the entrepreneurial, engineering and administrative problems are tackled in coherent, mutually complementary ways which enable the organization as a whole to survive.

In studies of a variety of kinds of organization Miles and Snow find four types of *adaptation strategies*, pursued by organizations, which they name Defenders, Prospectors, Analysers and Reactors. Defenders and Prospectors are at opposite ends of the continuum of possible strategies.

Analysers are somewhere in between, with some of the features of both. Each of these three types has its own typical solutions to the entrepreneurial, engineering and administrative problems. Reactors are different again. They seem unable to consistently pursue any of the other three types of strategy, reacting to events in an inconsistent way.

The first type, the *Defenders*, chooses to solve the entrepreneurial problem by aiming at a narrow and stable domain. They set themselves to sustain a prominent position in a narrow market segment, competing on either or both of quality and price to keep a particular clientele satisfied. They grow cautiously, step by step, by deeper penetration of this limited market. They reap the benefits of familiarity with it and with what they are doing, but tend to miss new developments because their managerial personnel has a restricted range of external contacts. There is a risk of their being caught by a major market shift in which they cannot adapt quickly enough.

Defenders are inclined to concentrate mostly on their engineering problem. Solving it is the key to their success. They succeed by being cost-efficient in doing what they know how to do well. They concentrate on improving quality control, production scheduling, materials handling and inventory control, distribution and the like. They buffer their core technology from external disturbance, as Thompson would put it, by carrying stocks of supplies and of products so that though there may be ups and downs in stocks, the production work itself can proceed steadily. Buffering may be helped through vertical integration with other organizations (i.e. by mutual ownership or contracts which ensure supplies and orders). However, while a Defender may work efficiently, here again there is a risk. It may be a long time before the investment in technology pays off.

Defender-type strategies lead to a typical administrative solution. Efficient supplying of a limited clientele requires relatively centralized control. Instructions flow down from the top, and reports and explanations flow upwards, via a 'long-looped vertical information system'. There is a central array of specialist departments, such as accounting, sales and personnel, administering a range of formalized documented procedures, such as budget returns, work schedules and stock listings. Together with the chief executive, the crucial finance and production functions dominate the centralized system. As always there are risks. While the system is orderly, novel opportunities may pass it by.

A Defender strategy has been pursued successfully by a food company in North California described by Miles and Snow. It has stayed within a speciality market for dried fruits and fruit juices. Beginning just by growing these, it met competition by extending into processing the fruit for consumption. This work has been mechanized, costs of growing fruit have been held down, and a small team specializes in improving quality. Control is centralized on the President and the heads of field operations, sales and finance, and higher than average wages ensure a stable labour force. The firm has a long-term coherence of entrepreneurial, engineering and administrative solutions.

The second type, *Prospectors*, the opposite of the Defenders, aims to find and exploit new opportunities. They stress 'doing the right things' rather than 'doing things right' as Defenders do. They may value a reputation for innovation more than they value profitability. Solving the entrepreneurial problem this way requires keeping in touch with trends and events across a wide field of view. A variety of individuals and sections in the organization bring in news of current happenings, not necessarily only the more obvious ones such as the market research or research and development departments. Growth comes from new products or services and from new markets, rather than from deeper penetration of the same market, as with a Defender. It is likely to occur in spurts, as opportunities are successfully taken up, rather than gradually. The gain to Prospectors from being open to fresh possibilities has to be balanced against the risks: that they may not be fully efficient in any one activity, and may over-extend themselves by taking on too much without sufficient recompense.

Their enterprising approach to the entrepreneurial problem requires a flexible solution to the engineering problem, so they use a variety of technologies. They do many things at once and can switch between them. Each line of work can be built up or discontinued fairly readily. There has to be trial and error work on prototypes. The gain is a flexible workforce; the cost is the difficulties of coordinating such a diversity of differing activity.

These solutions to the entrepreneurial and engineering problems are accompanied by a typical solution to the administrative problem. In the case of a Prospector, the administrative problem is how to facilitate all this activity, rather than how to control it. How can resources be deployed effectively without impeding the work by imposing inappropriately rigid central control? The answer is to plan broadly but not in detail. Skilled personnel can be relied on to know their jobs without detailed overseeing from the top. Small groups are gathered in project teams or task forces to work on new initiatives, and these, together with easy lateral contact between departments, create 'short horizontal feedback loops'. In other words, lines of communication are comparatively short. People can communicate quickly with anyone they need to contact without having to go to the top first. The structure is comparatively decentralized, and the marketing and the research and development functions are more influential than in a Defender. The advantage of this administrative solution overall is that it can respond rapidly to change, but inevitably there are risks. Some attempts to launch new products or services will be wasteful failures, costly both in capital and in the time of highly paid personnel.

Miles and Snow exemplify the Prospector strategy by relating the success of an electronics corporation. This huge enterprise, with 30,000 employees, makes and sells an extensive range of equipment, including small computers, calculators, electric meters and electrical testing equipment. Its entrepreneurial strategy is to keep one step ahead. There are frequent launches of new products with novelty value which fetch high prices. By the time prices fall, either the firm can manufacture cheaply just as its competitors have learned to, or another new launch is ready. Teams of scientists and engineers work on new possibilities, backed by the powerful marketing function whenever a new product is ready. The tendency is to create relatively autonomous divisions in each new product area. The company has a widely active and decentralized entrepreneurial, engineering and administrative pattern, quite different to the focused centralized Defender pattern.

Analysers attempt to achieve some of the strengths of both Defenders and Prospectors. They try to balance the minimizing of risk and the maximizing of profits. Their solution to the entrepreneurial problem is a mixture of stable and changing products and markets. Their stable activities generate earnings sufficient to enable them to move into innovative areas already opened up by Prospectors who have taken the early risks. The Analyser is a follower of change, not an initiator.

Since Analysers have something of both the Defender and of the Prospector entrepreneurial solutions, they are likely to have something of both engineering solutions. They are likely to have a dual technical core. That is, some of the work will be stable and routinized, while some will be shifting as new products are accepted and put into production quickly without the prolonged experimentation that a Prospector has to do. This combined solution to the engineering problem demands a corresponding dual administrative solution. There is both detailed control of stable lines and broad planning of innovations. Both production and marketing are influential, but so too, uniquely, are the personnel in applied research, since they are critical to getting new products into production. There are both central functional specialisms and also autonomous self-contained product groups.

Among examples of Analysers, Miles and Snow cite a medium-sized American general hospital. After many years of stability as a Defender it underwent a series of changes. These were intended to enable it to offer new services already offered by more innovative hospitals while still sustaining its traditional, relatively conventional, patient care. This change in solution to its entrepreneurial problem required it to move towards Prospector-type engineering and administrative solutions. While retaining existing medical technology, it acquired modern diagnostic equipment and the technical and medical staff to go with it. Administratively, its previous unitary structure was broken down into three semi-autonomous divisions, one of which contained all the new diagnostic services and clinics. It succeeded in following others into this kind of work, and in attracting a fresh range of lower-income patients, while keeping its established higher-income clientele.

Defenders, Prospectors and Analysers have viable strategies, but *Reactors* do not. They are an unstable form. They fail to achieve or hold to an appropriate defending, prospecting or analysing strategy. As a result, they are liable merely to react to change and to do so in ways that are both inconsistent and inappropriate, so they perform poorly. This makes them hesitant over what to do next. There are many possible reasons for this condition. Miles and Snow give examples of three. Perhaps the strategy is not 'articulated', so that managers are not fully aware of it, as sometimes happens when a strategy pursued successfully by a firm's founder dies with him and leaves the managers in disarray, not knowing what to do without him. Perhaps, even though there is a recognized strategy, the technology and the structure do not fit it, as when a publishing firm aspired to an Analyser strategy but could not separate its stable lines of work which needed careful central control from its changing lines which needed scope for trial and error. Possibly, both strategy and structure persist inappositely, as when a foods firm clung on to its long-established Defender strategy and structure even though declining profitability in a changing market pointed to the need for change.

Miles and Snow look beyond this typology of strategies to conjecture over signs of the future emergence of yet another type. This they call the *Market-Matrix* form of organization. It would 'pursue mixed strategies with mixed structures'. Some have moved towards it, from among recent kinds of organizations, such as conglomerates, multinational corporations, aerospace firms and certain educational institutions. They have matrix sections where lines of authority deliberately intersect or double up (e.g. where a department head also has responsibility for a major innovative project). A further step is then to expect such a project manager to bargain internally, market-fashion, for resources and for skilled personnel, the personnel having to be 'purchased' from existing departments. So a new form may be arising which is suited to complex tasks.

Miles and Snow intend their typology to help managers determine what kind of strategy to pursue. They present a Diagnostic Checklist of questions on an organization's present and potential strategies to use for this purpose.

BIBLIOGRAPHY

MILES, R. E., and SNOW, C. C., *Organizational Strategy, Structure and Process*, McGraw-Hill, 1978.

MILES, R. E., and SNOW, C. C., 'Fit, Failure and the Hall of Fame', *California Management Review*, 1984, 26, 10–28; reprinted in D. S. Pugh (ed.), *Organization Theory*, Penguin, 1997.

MILES, R. E., and SNOW, C. C., *Fit, Failure and the Hall of Fame*, Free Press, 1994.

Michael T. Hannan and John Freeman

Michael Hannan and John Freeman are both social scientists at Cornell University. After a period at Stanford University Hannan moved to Cornell, where his co-author Freeman had been for many years. Hannan is Scarborough Professor of Social Sciences. Freeman is Professor of Behavioural and Organizational Sciences and a former editor of the journal *Administrative Science Quarterly*.

It has been the shared aim of Hannan and Freeman to lift the view taken of organizations to a wider perspective. They have done this by looking at organizations much as a bioecologist or naturalist looks at animal life. They see populations of organizations surviving or thriving or declining in particular environments, just as populations of, say, rabbits survive or thrive in a particular ecological situation but die out in another. Just as the understanding of wildlife has been enhanced by the study of ecology, so can the understanding of organizations be enhanced. The wider ecological perspective goes beyond the problems each organization alone has in coping with the environment to see an organization as one of a population which coexists with or competes with other populations of organizations. The environment of each consists mainly of other organizations, so the existence of each is bound up with that of its own kind and of other kinds. Hence the *population ecology of organizations*.

Societies engage in many kinds of activities, and there are many different kinds of service and manufacturing organizations to do these activities. Why so many, and why does the number of different kinds rise and fall? This question is the same as 'Why are there so many species of animals?' and for both organizations and animals, population ecology explains the replacement of outmoded forms by new forms.

Indeed, the ability of a whole society to keep up with change depends upon the development of new forms of organization. If a society contains many differing forms of organization, then there is a good chance that one or more of these may fit some new circumstances which arise, and these new circumstances can then be taken advantage of quickly. If there are comparatively few forms of organization in a society, it has to adapt to change by modifying one or more of these or by creating a new form, and this takes longer. So a society that already has, among its hospitals, some which specialize in advanced surgery can readily add on heart transplant techniques; if it has only a uniform range of general hospitals dealing with the most common and cheaply treated ailments it has more difficulty in doing so.

This view assumes that populations of organizations evolve much as populations of biological species evolve. Those that fit their situation survive and thrive and those that do not die out. This is a 'Darwinian evolutionary position'. It argues that change takes place more by the growth of new forms of organization than by the intended reform of existing ones. Many theorists have pointed out that change in an organization is largely uncontrolled. Though its management may well believe that they are making changes according to plan, what happens is more haphazard than that. Differing views, unreliable information, and unforeseen eventualities make it uncertain whether they will get what they want, even if they know what they want (March p. 137, Thompson p. 68). Therefore, a Darwinian explanation that some forms fit the situation and prosper while others fail to fit and so decline is more tenable than supposing managements succeed in deliberately redesigning existing organizations to bring them up to date. Burns (p. 53) describes an example of this. Several well-established firms in Britain were unable to change sufficiently to move into the new field of electronics, though offered every encouragement to do so. Their form of organization was too fixed.

The evolution of populations of organizations is not necessarily a steady process. It is more likely that there are periods of rapid change as new forms are tried out, interspersed with comparative stability, during which existing forms persist. This would match contemporary views of biological evolution which regard it as 'punctuated equilibria' – long periods of comparatively balanced stability broken by shorter spasms of change. American labour unions did not grow steadily in number. There were spurts of activity at the end of the nineteenth century, again after the First World War, and again in the 1930s, when many new unions were founded. In between these peaks relatively few new ones appeared.

Hannan and Freeman concentrate on the density within each population (i.e. the number of organizations of a particular form). The density of a population is determined by how many organizations come and go. In other words, it is determined by how many are newly founded or come in from elsewhere, and by how many cease to exist or leave to do something different.

There are limits to density. Each *niche* in an environment can support a population density up to the limit of the *carrying capacity* of that niche. When the resources of a niche are exhausted, density can rise no further. That is, when competition for money and supplies and customers, or whatever else is needed, reaches an unsustainable level, some organizations will be squeezed out. This is analogous to what happens to wildlife when numbers become too great. Those who study wildlife regard a niche for insects or animals as 'the set of environmental conditions within which a population can grow or at least sustain its numbers'. In the niches inhabited by organizations, too, there is only room for so many.

Given these assumptions about organizations, Hannan and Freeman consider first how fast new organizations in a population are founded (the rate of *founding*), and then how fast they die out (the rate of *disbanding*). Consider founding. The fact that there are a growing number of a particular form of organization relative to the capacity of an environmental niche does not necessarily stop new entrants. Indeed, Hannan and Freeman contend that at first the rate of founding increases as density increases. The more there are, the more new ones attempt to get in. This is because a high density means more of that form of organization are around, so people become accustomed to them. Their existence is less likely to be questioned. They acquire greater legitimacy, as labour unions did after precarious early years when their right to exist was challenged. Further, the rate of new foundings may increase as total numbers grow also because there are more and more people who have experience of how to set up such an organization. The know-how is available. But there comes that level at which the niche can take no more, the level at which some are being squeezed out, and then launching new ones is no longer attractive. Then the rate of founding falls. So Hannan and Freeman argue that as the total number of organizations of a given form grows, first there are more new entrants and then there are fewer, because 'density increases legitimacy at a decreasing rate' but 'increases competition at an increasing rate'. If foundings are plotted against density, there should be an inverted U-shape.

This is shown in the United States in populations of organizations as different as labour unions, newspapers and semiconductor electronics firms. The history of unions and newspapers shows the pattern of first a rise and then a fall in foundings, while total numbers (density) increase, the pattern originating far back in the nineteenth century. Electronics is a much more recent and volatile population of the mid twentieth century. Here density increased rapidly as firms rushed to join this new industry, and so competition forced down the rate of entry to the industry much more quickly than was the case with the unions and newspapers.

Disbanding, or 'mortality', is held to be the other way around. As the total number of organizations in a population grows, there are first fewer disbandings and then more. Of course, the number of disbandings, the 'fatalities' in a population through closures or withdrawals from their field, may actually start quite high for the same reason that foundings start low, because legitimacy and know-how are hard to get when few of a kind exist. But the rate of disbandings soon drops as survival becomes easier, and so there are fewer and fewer disbandings, and more and more survivors. Once again, however, when density reaches a level where the niche can support no more, the trend changes. It swings round from a falling rate of disbandings to an increasing rate. Competition forces organizations out, and the number of disbandings begins to rise and may go on rising as long as density goes on rising.

Plotting disbandings against density should produce a U-shaped curve. So indeed it did for the unions, newspapers and electronics populations. The rate of disbanding dropped sharply for all three as their total numbers increased, and then rose again under the pressure of competition. But the force of competitive pressure appeared to differ. It seemed weakest for newspapers, stronger for electronics firms, and strongest for unions, which squeezed each other out more and more once the critical density of union population was reached. The existence of a large number of craft unions, with members from the same occupations in many industries, seemed detrimental, especially to industrial unions with members from many oc-cupations in a single industry, for as the density of craft unions rose, so too did the disbanding of industrial unions.

Disbandings are also influenced by age and size of organization. Hannan and Freeman do not agree with assertions that modern organizations are (or should be) in a state of constant flux and innovation. As they see it, organizations persist because of their reliability in outputs of goods and services and their accountability for the use of resources, each of which increases with institutionalization and stability. So the stability of age improves the chances of survival, despite the inertia that ageing can bring. There are fewer disbandings in populations of older organizations. Older unions and older firms are less likely to close down or merge than are younger ones.

Growth, too, improves the chances. Although bigger organizations similarly may have greater structural inertia, they have the resources to withstand shocks from their environments. 'Small organizations are more likely than large ones to attempt change, but are more likely to disappear in the process.'

Within populations, sub-populations are found to respond differently to different environmental niche conditions. Thus among both restaurants and semiconductor firms, generalists (with a relatively wide range of services or products) are found to do better under variable conditions. Specialists (with a narrower range) do better in stable cyclical conditions, called coarse-grained environments (where there are known long-term business cycles). In further work Hannan and his colleague Glenn Carroll show that these characteristics also apply to other niches. These include the American brewing and banking industries and the population of newspapers in both Argentina and Ireland.

As applied to organizations by Hannan and Freeman, population ecology theory questions the usefulness of the efforts commonly made to reform existing organizations as managements attempt to keep up with change. It implies that populations of organizations or particular organizations change more effectively by selection and replacement than by adaptation. To effect change, start a new organization.

Here population ecology theory becomes practical, for potentially it can show whether 'the dice are loaded for or against a particular way of doing business.' There is no best form of organization, but many forms for many niches.

BIBLIOGRAPHY

HANNAN M. T., and FREEMAN, J., 'The Population Ecology of Organizations', *American Journal of Sociology*, 1977, 82, 929–64; reprinted in D. S. Pugh (ed.), *Organization Theory*, Penguin, 1997.

HANNAN, M. T., and FREEMAN, J., *Organizational Ecology*, Harvard University Press, 1989.

HANNAN, M. T., and CARROLL, G. R., *Dynamics of Organizational Populations*, Oxford University Press, 1992.

Geert Hofstede

Geert Hofstede is a social psychologist who until his retirement was Professor of Organizational Anthropology and International Management at the University of Limburg, the Netherlands, and Director of the Institute for Research on Inter-Cultural Cooperation there. In the early 1970s he and his colleagues carried out a major systematic study of work-related attitudes based on two questionnaire surveys, which produced a total of over 116,000 questionnaires from over seventy countries around the world – making it by far the largest organizationally based study ever to have been carried out.

Those respondents whose replies were used by Hofstede for research purposes were all sales and service employees of subsidiaries of IBM – a US-based multinational corporation which operates in most countries in the world. Within the sales and service function all types of employees were surveyed – sales clerks, professional engineers, top managers, etc. – using the language of each country. A total of twenty different language versions of the questionnaire had to be made. The IBM employees represented well-matched sub-sets from each country: same company, job and education but different nationalities. National cultural differences found within the company, therefore, are likely to be a conservative estimate of those existing within the countries at large. The survey was repeated after four years with stable results, underlining the persistent cultural nature of the differences found.

Hofstede identifies four basic dimensions of the differences between national cultures based on the forty larger subsidiaries on which the first analyses were made. Each of the national cultures can be positioned from high to low on each of the four scales, and thus has a distinctive cultural profile. The four dimensions are:

1. Power–distance
2. Uncertainty–avoidance

3. Individualism
4. Masculinity

The power–distance dimension is concerned with how close or how distant subordinates feel from their superiors. This is not physical distance, but how big the personal gap is felt to be. In a high power–distance culture (e.g. France, India) being a boss means exerting power and keeping that gap open. Inequality is accepted: 'a place for everyone and everyone in their place'. So employees are frequently reluctant to express disagreement with their bosses and prefer to work for managers who take the decisions – and the responsibility – and then simply tell them what to do.

In a low power distance culture (e.g. Austria, Israel) superiors and subordinates consider each other to be colleagues, and both believe that inequalities in society should be minimized. So those in power should try to look less powerful than they are. Employees are seldom afraid to disagree and expect to be consulted before decisions are made.

The uncertainty–avoidance dimension is the ease with which the culture copes with novelty. In strong uncertainty–avoidance cultures (e.g. Japan, Greece) people feel the need for clarity and order. They feel threatened by uncertain situations, and higher anxiety and stress are experienced. This is combated by hard work, career stability and intolerance of deviancy. Thus employees believe that company rules should not be broken – even when it is shown to be in the company's best interest – and look forward to continue working with the firm until they retire.

In a weak uncertainty–avoidance culture (e.g. Denmark, Hong Kong) the uncertainty inherent in life is more easily accepted and each day is taken as it comes. A very pragmatic view is taken about keeping or changing those rules which are in existence, and employees expect to be working for the firm for much shorter periods.

The individualism dimension focuses on the degree to which the culture encourages individual as opposed to collectivist, group-centred concerns. In an individualist culture (e.g. USA, Britain) the emphasis is on personal initiative and achievement, and everyone has the right to a private life and opinion. By contrast, a collectivist culture (e.g. Iran, Peru) is characterized by a tighter social framework, where people are members of extended families or clans which protect them in exchange for loyalty. Careers are pursued to increase standing in the family by being able to help other members of it. The emphasis is on belonging and the aim is to be a good member – whereas in the individualist culture the ideal is to be a good leader.

The masculinity dimension highlights 'masculine' cultures (e.g. Australia, Italy) where performance is what counts; money and material standards are important, ambition is the driving force. Big and fast are beautiful; 'machismo' is sexy. In contrast, in 'feminine' cultures (e.g. the Netherlands, Sweden) it is the quality of life that matters: people and the environment are important, service provides the motivation, small is beautiful and unisex is attractive. The expected relationship of men to women differs considerably along this dimension. In 'masculine' cultures the sex roles are clearly differentiated. Men should be assertive, dominating; women should be caring, nurturing. In 'feminine' cultures the sex roles are more flexible, and there is a belief in equality between the sexes. It is not 'unmasculine' for a man to take a caring role, for example.

Equipped with measurements which locate the forty cultures along the four dimensions, Hofstede then offers a set of cultural maps of the world. Two points should be remembered in interpreting the results. The first is that countries spread along the whole of each of the four dimensions, not only at the extremes. So cultures are not only masculine like Italy or feminine like Sweden; there are also many countries in between: Belgium exactly in the centre; Britain on the masculine side, France on the feminine one.

The second point to remember is that the position of a culture along a dimension is based on the averages for all the respondents in that particular country. Characterizing a national work culture does not mean that every person in the nation has all the characteristics ascribed to that culture – there are bound to be many individual variations. There are, for example, many Japanese who are risk-takers and many from Hong Kong who avoid uncertainty; many Indians with low power–distance values and many Israelis with high power–distance attitudes. What these scales are doing is describing the common values of the central core of the culture which come about through the 'collective mental programming' of a number of people (a tribe, a nation or a national minority) who are conditioned by the same life experience and the same education. Although this will not make everybody the same, a country's nationals do share a cultural character – which is indeed more clearly visible to foreigners than to themselves.

The table (opposite) gives a classification of the nations grouped by

Country clusters and their characteristics

I: More developed Latin	II: Less developed Latin
high power–distance	high power–distance
high uncertainty–avoidance	high uncertainty–avoidance
medium to high individualism	low individualism
medium masculinity	whole range on masculinity
BELGIUM	COLOMBIA
FRANCE	MEXICO
ARGENTINA	VENEZUELA
BRAZIL	CHILE
SPAIN	PERU
(ITALY)	PORTUGAL

III: More developed Asian	IV: Less developed Asian	V: Near Eastern
medium power–distance	high power–distance	high power–distance
high uncertainty–avoidance	low to medium uncertainty–avoidance	high uncertainty–avoidance
medium individualism	low individualism	low individualism
high masculinity	medium masculinity	medium masculinity
JAPAN	PAKISTAN	GREECE
	TAIWAN	IRAN
	THAILAND	TURKEY
	HONG KONG	(YUGOSLAVIA)
	INDIA	
	PHILIPPINES	
	SINGAPORE	

VI: Germanic	VII: Anglo	VIII: Nordic
low power–distance	low to medium power–distance	low power–distance
medium to high uncertainty–avoidance	low to medium uncertainty–avoidance	low to medium uncertainty–avoidance
medium individualism	high individualism	medium to high individualism
medium to high masculinity	high masculinity	low masculinity
AUSTRIA	AUSTRALIA	DENMARK
ISRAEL	CANADA	FINLAND
GERMANY	BRITAIN	NETHERLANDS
SWITZERLAND	IRELAND	NORWAY
	NEW ZEALAND	SWEDEN
	USA	
	(SOUTH AFRICA)	

from Hofstede (1980)

cultural similarity according to the statistical technique of cluster analysis. They fall into eight areas. Since a culture's work-related values are so distinctive and different, it is to be expected that its organizational processes and behaviour would be so too. So Hofstede argues very strongly that we should not expect the same conceptions and prescriptions about management to be appropriate for all culture areas.

Some years later Hofstede joined Michael Bond, a Canadian social psychologist working in Hong Kong, in research which added a fifth dimension to the previous four. Bond, realizing that most questionnaires have questions devised by Westerners, as did Hofstede's IBM surveys, investigated what would happen if the questions were developed by Asians. He asked Chinese social scientists in Hong Kong and Taiwan to define some Chinese cultural values. From these a questionnaire was made up in Chinese and then translated into English and other languages – the other way round from the usual practice. The questionnaire was given to matched sets of students in different countries, East and West.

The most compelling finding was that three of the dimensions obtained were compatible with those found previously. Power–distance, individualism and masculinity again differentiated among the national groups. The most distinctive finding was that a new dimension replaced Hofstede's, possibly Western-biased, uncertainty–avoidance. It distinguishes cultures in which persistence, thrift and a firm status order in society, plus a keen sense of shame, are much more important than are respect for tradition, saving face socially, personal steadiness and mutual honouring of favours and gifts. In so far as what is most important is more forward-looking, Bond called this Eastern-orientated characteristic *Confucian Dynamism*. Hofstede subsequently preferred to call it long-term versus short-term orientation.

Remarkably, all the most vigorous Asian economies – Japan, Taiwan, South Korea, Hong Kong, Singapore, and China itself – were high in Confucian Dynamism, i.e. had a long-term orientation. Could this element in the cultures of their peoples partly explain their economic success, much as the so-called Protestant work ethic of earlier centuries in the West has been held to partly explain the Industrial Revolution (see Weber, p. 8)?

Hofstede illustrates the difficulties of applying management practices insensitively in very different cultures by what befell an American idea when attempts were made to introduce it elsewhere. Management by

Objectives (MbO) started in the United States and has had most success there, particularly in situations where the manager's results can be objectively measured. Why is this so? MbO requires that:

1. Subordinates are sufficiently independent to negotiate meaningfully with the boss (i.e. low power–distance).
2. Both are willing to take some risks – the boss in delegating power, the subordinate in accepting responsibility (i.e. low uncertainty–avoidance).
3. The subordinate is personally willing to 'have a go' and make a mark (i.e. high individualism).
4. Both regard performance and results achieved as important (i.e. high masculinity).

This is the Anglo work culture pattern as the table shows.

But how would MbO work out in other culture areas? For example, the Germanic culture area has low power–distance which fits, as do the results orientation of high masculinity. However, the Germanic group is high on uncertainty–avoidance which would work against the risk-taking and ambiguity involved in the Anglo process. But the idea of replacing the arbitrary authority of the boss with the impersonal authority of mutually agreed objectives fits well in this culture. This is, indeed, the way MbO has developed in Germany, emphasizing the need to develop procedures of a more participative kind. The German name for MbO is 'Management by Joint Goal Setting', and elaborate formal systems have been developed. There is also great stress on team objectives (as opposed to the individual emphasis in the Anglo culture) and this fits in with the lower individualism of this culture area.

The more developed Latin group, as represented by France, has high power–distance and high uncertainty–avoidance – completely the opposite to the Anglo group – so MbO is bound to encounter difficulties there. It did gain some popularity in France for a time, but it was not sustained. The problem was that in a high power–distance culture attempting to substitute the personal authority of the boss by self-monitored objectives is bound to generate anxiety. The boss does not delegate easily and will not stop short-circuiting intermediate hierarchical levels if necessary – and subordinates will expect this to happen and to be told what to do. And in a high uncertainty–avoidance culture, anxiety will be alleviated by sticking to the old ways.

Cultural differences, then, have an important impact on how organizations function, and manufacturing cars or treating the sick will call for different structures and processes in France or Japan or Britain. So it is important even for international organizations to have a dominant national culture to fall back on (e.g. as the American or Japanese multinationals). Organizations without a home culture, in which the key decision-makers can come from any country (e.g. UNESCO, the EU Commission), find it very difficult to function effectively because of this lack. It is less of a problem for the political part of such organizations, since negotiation between representatives is their task. But for the administrative apparatus, where the members represent not their countries but the organization as a whole, it is crippling – and most such 'cultureless' organizations are inefficient and wasteful.

BIBLIOGRAPHY

HOFSTEDE, G., *Culture's Consequences*, Sage Publications, 1980.

HOFSTEDE, G., 'Motivation, Leadership and Organization: Do American Theories Apply Abroad?', *Organizational Dynamics* (Summer, 1980), 42–63; reprinted in D. S. Pugh (ed.), *Organization Theory*, Penguin, 1997.

HOFSTEDE, G., *Cultures and Organizations: Software of the Mind*, McGraw-Hill, 1991.

THREE

The Management of Organizations

To manage is to forecast and plan, to organize, to command, to coordinate and to control.
HENRI FAYOL

Scientific management will mean, for the employers and the workmen who adopt it, the elimination of almost all causes for dispute and disagreement between them.
FREDERICK W. TAYLOR

It [modern management] was to ensure that as a craft declined the worker would sink to the level of general and undifferentiated labour power, adaptable to a large range of simple tasks, while as science grew, it would be concentrated in the hands of management.
HARRY BRAVERMAN

Excellent companies were, above all, brilliant on the basics.
THOMAS J. PETERS and ROBERT H. WATERMAN

The degree to which the opportunity to use power effectively is granted or withheld from individuals is one operative difference between those companies which stagnate and those which innovate.
ROSABETH MOSS KANTER

An organization . . . quite literally does impose the environment that imposes on it.
KARL E. WEICK

Organizations with different structures, functioning in different environments, have to be managed. As long as there is management there will be the problem of how to manage better. In one sense, attempts at answers to the problem will be as numerous as there are managers, for each will bring an individual approach to the task. None the less, at any one time there is enough in common for there to be broad similarities in what is thought and what is taught on this issue. The writers in this section have each sought to improve the understanding of administration and its practice. They have looked for the ingredients of a better management.

Henri Fayol puts forward a classic analysis of the management task, based on his long practical experience of doing the job, and the personal insights he gained. F. W. Taylor's name is synonymous with the term 'scientific management'. His extremely influential ideas made him a controversial figure in his own day and have remained a subject for much argument. Harry Braverman, from a Marxist perspective, mounts a critique on the degradation which Taylor's ideas bring to modern work. Thomas Peters and Robert Waterman, in an influential analysis, report a set of attributes which characterize excellent firms and propose that they should be widely adopted. Rosabeth Moss Kanter proposes ways in which organizations should be managed to draw more fully on the total human resources within them. Karl E. Weick points to the way in which each individual's subjective attempts to make sense of the organization must be understood and taken into account in the management process.

Henri Fayol

Henri Fayol (1841–1925) was a mining engineer by training. A Frenchman, he spent his working life with the French mining and metallurgical combine Commentry-Fourchamboult-Decazeville, first as an engineer, but from his early thirties onwards in general management. From 1888 to 1918 he was Managing Director.

Fayol is among those who have achieved fame for ideas made known very late in his life. He was in his seventies before he published them in a form which came to be widely read. He had written technical articles on mining engineering and a couple of preliminary papers on administration, but it was in 1916 that the *Bulletin de la Société de l'Industrie Minérale* printed Fayol's *Administration Industrielle et Générale – Prévoyance, Organisation, Commandement, Coordination, Contrôle.* He is also among those whose reputation rests on a single short publication still frequently reprinted as a book; his other writings are little known.

The English version appears as *General and Industrial Management*, translated by Constance Storrs and first issued in 1949. There has been some debate over this rendering of the title of the work, and in particular of expressing the French word '*administration*' by the term 'management'. It is argued that this could simply imply that Fayol is concerned only with industrial management, whereas his own preface claims that: 'Management plays a very important part in the government of undertakings; of all undertakings, large or small, industrial, commercial, political, religious or any other.' Indeed, in his last years he studied the problems of State public services and lectured at the *École Supérieure de la Guerre.* So it can be accepted that his intention was to initiate a theoretical analysis appropriate to a wide range of organizations.

Fayol suggests that: 'All activities to which industrial undertakings give rise can be divided into the following groups:

1. Technical activities (production, manufacture, adaptation).

2. Commercial activities (buying, selling, exchange).
3. Financial activities (search for and optimum use of capital).
4. Security activities (protection of property and persons).
5. Accounting activities (stocktaking, balance sheet, costs, statistics).
6. Managerial activities (planning, organization, command, coordination, control).

Be the undertaking simple or complex, big or small, these six groups of activities or essential functions are always present.'

Most of these six groups of activities will be present in most jobs, but in varying measure, with the managerial element in particular being greatest in senior jobs and least or absent in direct production or lower clerical tasks. Managerial activities are specially emphasized as being universal to organizations. But it is a commonplace to ask: What is management? Is it anything that can be identified and stand on its own, or is it a word, a label, that has no substance?

Fayol's answer was unique at the time. The core of his contribution is his definition of management as comprising five elements:

1. To forecast and plan (in the French, *prévoyance*): 'examining the future and drawing up the plan of action'.
2. To organize: 'building up the structure, material and human, of the undertaking'.
3. To command: 'maintaining activity among the personnel'.
4. To coordinate: 'binding together, unifying and harmonizing all activity and effort'.
5. To control: 'seeing that everything occurs in conformity with established rule and expressed command'.

For Fayol, managing means looking ahead, which makes the process of *forecasting and planning* a central business activity. Management must 'assess the future and make provision for it'. To function adequately a business organization needs a plan which has the characteristics of 'unity, continuity, flexibility and precision'. The problems of planning which management must overcome are: making sure that the objectives of each part of the organization are securely welded together (unity); using both short- and long-term forecasting (continuity); being able to adapt the plan in the light of changing circumstances (flexibility); and attempting to accurately predict courses of action (precision). The essence of planning is to allow the optimum use of resources. Interestingly, Fayol in 1916 argued the necessity of a national plan for France, to be produced by the government.

To *organize* is 'building up the structure, material and human, of the undertaking'. The task of management is to build up an organization which will allow the basic activities to be carried out in an optimal manner. Central to this is a structure in which plans are efficiently prepared and carried out. There must be unity of command and direction, clear definition of responsibilities, precise decision-making backed up by an efficient system for selecting and training managers.

Fayol's third element comes logically after the first two. An organization must start with a plan, a definition of its goals. It then must produce an organization structure appropriate to the achievement of those goals. Third, the organization must be put in motion, which is *command*, maintaining activity among the personnel. Through an ability to command, the manager obtains the best possible performance from subordinates. This must be done through example, knowledge of the business, knowledge of the subordinates, continuous contact with staff, and by maintaining a broad view of the directing function. In this way the manager maintains a high level of activity by instilling a sense of mission.

Command refers to the relationship between a manager and the subordinates in the area of the immediate task. But organizations have a variety of tasks to perform, so *coordination* is necessary 'binding together, unifying and harmonizing all activity and effort'. Essentially this is making sure that one department's efforts are coincident with the efforts of other departments, and keeping all activities in perspective with regard to the overall aims of the organization. This can only be attained by a constant circulation of information and regular meetings of management.

Finally there is *control*, logically the final element which checks that the other four elements are in fact performing properly: 'seeing that everything occurs in conformity with established rule and expressed command.' To be effective, control must operate quickly and there must be a system of sanctions. The best way to ensure this is to separate all functions concerned with inspection from the operation departments whose work they inspect. Fayol believed in independent, impartial staff departments.

Fayol uses this classification to divide up his chapters on how to administer or manage. It is probable that when he wrote of '*une doctrine administrative*' he had in mind not only the above theory but the addition of experience to theoretical analysis to form a doctrine of good management. He summarizes the lessons of his own experience in a number of General Principles of Management. These are his own rules and he does not assume they are necessarily of universal application nor that they have any great permanence. None the less, most have become part of managerial know-how and many are regarded as fundamental tenets. Fayol outlines the following fourteen principles:

1. Division of work: specialization allows the individual to build up expertise and thereby be more productive.
2. Authority: the right to issue commands, along with which must go the equivalent responsibility for its exercise.
3. Discipline: which is two-sided, for employees only obey orders if management play their part by providing good leadership.
4. Unity of command: in contrast to F. W. Taylor's functional authority (see p. 105), Fayol was quite clear that each worker should have only one boss with no other conflicting lines of command. On this issue history has favoured Fayol, for his principle has found most adherents among managers.
5. Unity of direction: people engaged in the same kind of activities must have the same objectives in a single plan.
6. Subordination of individual interest to general interest: management must see that the goals of the firm are always paramount.
7. Remuneration: payment is an important motivator although, by ana-lysing a number of different possibilities, Fayol points out that there is no such thing as a perfect system.
8. Centralization or decentralization: again this is a matter of degree depending on the condition of the business and the quality of its personnel.
9. Scalar chain: a hierarchy is necessary for unity of direction but lateral communication is also fundamental as long as superiors know that such communication is taking place.
10. Order: both material order and social order are necessary. The former minimizes lost time and useless handling of materials. The latter is achieved through organization and selection.
11. Equity: in running a business, a 'combination of kindliness and justice' is needed in treating employees if equity is to be achieved.
12. Stability of tenure: this is essential due to the time and expense

involved in training good management. Fayol believes that successful businesses tend to have more stable managerial personnel.

13. Initiative: allowing all personnel to show their initiative in some way is a source of strength for the organization even though it may well involve a sacrifice of 'personal vanity' on the part of many managers.

14. *Esprit de corps*: management must foster the morale of its employees and, to quote Fayol, 'real talent is needed to coordinate effort, encourage keenness, use each person's abilities, and reward each one's merit without arousing possible jealousies and disturbing harmonious relations.'

But Fayol's pride of place in this field is due not so much to his principles of how to manage, enduring though these are, as to his definition of what management is. He is the earliest known proponent of a theoretical analysis of managerial activities – an analysis which has withstood a half century of critical discussion. There can have been few writers since who have not been influenced by it; and his five elements have provided a system of concepts with which managers may clarify their thinking about what it is they have to do.

BIBLIOGRAPHY

FAYOL, H., *General and Industrial Management*, Pitman, 1949. Translated by Constance Storrs from the original *Administration Industrielle et Générale*, 1916.

Frederick W. Taylor

Frederick Winslow Taylor (1856–1917) was an engineer by training. He joined the Midvale Steel Works as a labourer and rose rapidly to be foreman and later Chief Engineer. He was afterwards employed at the Bethlehem Steel Works, then became a consultant and devoted his time to the propagation of his ideas.

He first published his views on management in a paper entitled 'A piece rate system', read to the American Society of Mechanical Engineers in 1895. These views were expanded into a book, *Shop Management* (1903), and further developed in *Principles of Scientific Management* (1911). As a result of labour troubles caused by the attempt to apply his principles in a government arsenal, a House of Representatives Special Committee was set up in 1911 to investigate Taylor's system of shop management. (A full description of events at the arsenal is given in Aitken's case study.) In 1947, *Shop Management*, the *Principles*, and Taylor's Testimony to the Special Committee were collected together and published under the title of *Scientific Management*.

Taylor was the founder of the movement known as 'scientific management'. 'The principal object of management', he states, 'should be to secure the maximum prosperity for the employer, coupled with the maximum prosperity of each employee.' For the employer, 'maximum prosperity' means not just large profits in the short term but the development of all aspects of the enterprise to a state of permanent prosperity. For the employees 'maximum prosperity' means not just immediate higher wages, but their development so that they may perform efficiently in the highest grade of work for which their natural abilities fit them. The mutual interdependence of management and workers, and the necessity of their working together towards the common aim of increased prosperity for all seemed completely self-evident to Taylor. He was thus driven to asking: Why is there so much antagonism and inefficiency?

He suggests three causes: first, the fallacious belief of the workers that any increase in output would inevitably result in unemployment; second, the defective systems of management which make it necessary for workers to restrict output in order to protect their interests ('systematic soldiering'); third, inefficient rule-of-thumb, effort-wasting methods of work. Taylor conceived it to be the aim of 'scientific management' to overcome these obstacles. This could be achieved by a systematic study of work to discover the most efficient methods of performing the job, and then a systematic study of management leading to the most efficient methods of controlling the workers. This would bring a great increase in efficiency and with it prosperity to the benefit of all, since a highly efficient prosperous business would be in a much better position to ensure the continuing well-paid employment of its workers. As Taylor put it: 'What the workmen want from their employers beyond anything else is high wages and what employers want from their workmen most of all is low labour cost of manufacture . . . the existence or absence of these two elements forms the best index to either good or bad management.'

To achieve this Taylor lays down four 'great underlying principles of management':

THE DEVELOPMENT OF A TRUE SCIENCE OF WORK

He points out that we do not really know what constitutes a fair day's work; a boss therefore has unlimited opportunities for complaining about workers' inadequacies, and workers never really know what is expected of them. This can be remedied by the establishment after scientific investigation of a 'large daily task' as the amount to be done by a suitable worker under optimum conditions. For this they would receive a high rate of pay – much higher than the average worker would receive in 'unscientific' factories. They would also suffer a loss of income if they failed to achieve this performance.

THE SCIENTIFIC SELECTION AND PROGRESSIVE DEVELOPMENT OF THE WORKER

To earn this high rate of pay workers would have to be scientifically selected to ensure that they possess the physical and intellectual qualities to enable them to achieve the output. Then they must be systematically trained to be 'first-class'. Taylor believes that every worker could be first-class at some job. It was the responsibility of management to develop workers, offering them opportunities for advancement which would finally enable them to do 'the highest, most interesting and most profitable class of work' for which they could become 'first-class'.

THE BRINGING TOGETHER OF THE SCIENCE OF WORK AND THE SCIENTIFICALLY SELECTED AND TRAINED WORKERS

It is this process that causes the 'mental revolution' in management and Taylor maintains that almost invariably the major resistance to scientific management comes from the side of management. The workers, he finds, are very willing to cooperate in learning to do a good job for a high rate of pay.

THE CONSTANT AND INTIMATE COOPERATION OF MANAGEMENT AND WORKERS

There is an almost equal division of work and responsibility between management and workers. The management takes over all the work for which they are better fitted than the workers, i.e. the specification and verification of the methods, time, price and quality standards of the job, and the continuous supervision and control of the workers doing it. As Taylor saw it, there should be hardly a single act done by any worker which is not preceded by and followed by some act on the part of management. With this close personal cooperation the opportunities for conflict are almost eliminated, since the operation of this authority is not arbitrary. The managers are continually demonstrating that their decisions are subject to the same discipline as the workers, namely the scientific study of the work.

By 'science' Taylor means systematic observation and measurement, and an example of his method that he often quotes is the development of 'the science of shovelling'. He is insistent that, although shovelling is a very simple job, the study of the factors affecting efficient shovelling is quite complex. So much so that a worker who is phlegmatic enough to be able to do the job and stupid enough to choose it is extremely unlikely to be able to develop the most efficient method alone. But this is in fact what is hoped will happen. The *scientific* study of shovelling involves the determination of the optimum load that a 'first-class' worker can handle with each shovelful. Then the correct size of shovel to obtain this load, with different materials, must be established. Workers must be provided with a range of shovels and told which one to use. They must then be placed on an incentive payment scheme which allows them to earn high wages (double what they would earn in 'unscientific' firms) in return for high output.

The insistence on maximum specialization and the removal of all extraneous elements in order to concentrate on the essential task, is fundamental to Taylor's thinking. He applies this concept to management too. He considers that the work of a typical factory supervisor is composed of a number of different functions (such as cost clerk, time clerk, inspector, repair boss, shop disciplinarian) and he believes that these could be separated out and performed by different specialists who would each be responsible for controlling different aspects of the work and the workers. He calls this system 'functional management' and likens the increased efficiency that it would bring to that obtained in a school where classes go to specialist teachers for different subjects, compared with a school in which one teacher teaches all subjects. He also formulates 'the exception principle' which lays down that management reports should be condensed into comparative summaries giving in detail only the exceptions to past standards or averages – both the especially good and the especially bad exceptions. Thus the manager would obtain an immediate and comprehensive view of the progress of the work.

Taylor's methods have been followed by many others, among them Gantt, Frank and Lillian Gilbreth, Bedaux, Rowan and Halsey. They have developed his thinking into what is now called Work Study or Industrial Engineering. But even in his lifetime Taylor's ideas led to bitter controversy over the alleged inhumanity of his system, which was said to reduce workers to the level of efficiently functioning machines. In fairness to Taylor, it must be said that his principles were often inadequately understood. For example, few managements have been willing to put into practice one of his basic tenets – that there should be no limit to the earnings of a high-producing worker; many incentive schemes involve such limits. This may inhibit the 'mental revolution' Taylor sought, which requires that 'both sides take their eyes off the division of the surplus as the all important matter and together turn their attention towards increasing the size of the surplus.'

BIBLIOGRAPHY

TAYLOR, F. W., *Scientific Management*, Harper & Row, 1947.
AITKEN, H. G. J., *Taylorism at Watertown Arsenal*, Harvard University Press, 1960.

Harry Braverman and the 'Labour Process' Debate

Harry Braverman (1920–76) was an American Marxist theorist who was concerned to analyse the effects of the modern capitalist economy on the organization of work. He was stimulated to this by what he regarded as the unrealistic nature of much of what was written about productive labour. Braverman himself had very practical experience to bring to his analysis: he was trained as a craftsman coppersmith, and worked at that trade and at pipe-fitting and sheet-metal work. He was employed in a naval shipyard, a railroad repair shop and two sheet-steel plants – in all of which he experienced the impact of technological change on craft employment. In later years as a journalist, book editor, then publishing executive, he again had experience of the impact of modern technology, this time on administrative work such as marketing, accounting and book production routines. His basic thesis is that in a capitalist economy all these changes act to de-skill work and to remove more and more power away from workers and into the hands of owners and managers. His book expounding this theme, *Labour and Monopoly Capitalism: the Degradation of Work in the Twentieth Century*, was awarded the 1974 C. Wright Mills Prize of the Society for the Study of Social Problems.

Braverman uses the framework for analysing the nature of the capitalist system presented by Karl Marx in *Capital*, Volume 1 (published in 1867), and applies it to modern work and its organization. Marx used the term the 'labour process' to refer to the ways by which raw materials are transformed into goods by human labour using tools and machines. In a capitalist system, by definition, the tools and machines are not owned by the workers but by the capitalists, and so the resulting goods become commodities to be sold on the market for the owners' profit. Workers themselves also have only a commodity to offer: their labour in exchange for wages. In this system it is inevitable that owners will 'exploit' workers (i.e. obtain as much as possible as a contribution to profit while paying as little as possible in return as wages).

In modern terms, according to Braverman, this requires managers (as representatives of owners) to design and redesign work in order to achieve competitive levels of profit. They need to have maximum control of workers and to be looking continually for ways of increasing that control. Typically, this has been achieved by increasing the division of labour into smaller and smaller, less and less demanding fragments of tasks. In this way increased output may be obtained from a workforce which is cheaper, since it is less skilled and less trained. Ford-type mass production epitomizes the results. Car workers on an assembly line, for example, who drive to their place of work, will have already exercised their highest level of skill for that day.

This de-skilling and the abolition of craft ownership of work leads to alienation. This is another reason for the owning class (and its representatives – the managers) to need to control the working class. They are seen as untrustworthy members of an opposing class who are likely to obstruct, undermine or otherwise resist the legitimate capitalist objective of maximizing profit. From this point of view, ways of organizing the labour and production process are not rationally determined in order to increase objective efficiency: rather, organizations take the form they do in order to enhance the domination of capital over labour.

The prime advocate of this approach to efficiency in the organization of production was F. W. Taylor (see p. 102). Braverman sees 'Scientific Management', so-called, as the classic and inevitable method used to control labour in growing capitalist enterprises. It is, of course, not scientific since it does not attempt to discover what is the actual case, but accepts management's view that it has a refractory workforce which has to be kept under control. It is not a 'science of work' but a 'science of the management of others' work under capitalist conditions'. Its three basic tenets are: that knowledge of the labour process must be gathered in one place, that it must be the exclusive preserve of management and not available to the workers, and that this monopoly of knowlege must be used by management to control each step of the labour process. In total contrast to craft working, Taylor advocated a complete separation of conception from execution.

Braverman insists that Scientific Management is in full flow as the dominant approach to capitalist organization of the labour process. He is very dismissive of those social science writers of the 'human relations' approach (see Mayo p. 157, Likert and McGregor p. 161, Herzberg p. 172, etc.) who maintain the need to humanize work and improve the quality of working life. In industry these ideas are relegated to the sidelines of the personnel and training departments, with little real impact on the management of worker or work. In the production departments where the labour process is actually carried out and controlled, Taylorism reigns supreme. It is indeed being extended to an even wider range of occupations, such as clerical and administrative routines, which are continually being de-skilled with the use of new computer technology. Braverman rejects the idea that automation is qualitatively different in the skill demands it makes of workers, as compared to mechanization. He argues that it, too, will decrease skill, as will any other technological development. This result is not a matter of a particular technology, but of how it is inevitably used to increase the control of the labour process by capital in the interests of profit.

The de-skilling, and cheapening, of such 'white collar' jobs as those of clerks and computer operators, leads to an increase in the alienated working class. In the situation of 'monopoly capitalism' (i.e. where giant corporations control the markets), new commodities are brought into being to shape the consumer to the needs of capital. All of society becomes a gigantic market place in the pursuit of profit. Printing and television, for example, become vehicles largely for marketing rather than for information and education. Thus, there is not only the degradation of work but also the degradation of family and community.

In the aftermath of Braverman's book, Marxist sociologists have been discussing its adequacy. Two particular issues have been taken up. The first concerns the inevitability of de-skilling on Taylorist lines in capitalist production. Braverman argued that it was the one classic form which gave cheapness and control in the labour process, and therefore was the inevitable result. Later writers have suggested that de-skilling may not be universal and work under capitalism can take a variety of forms. Managements may use different ways to achieve their objectives of control. Richard Edwards in an historical survey of workplace relations, argues that, although a hierarchy has remained constant, various additional forms of control have been used (e.g. coercive, technical, bureaucratic), depending upon the struggle of owners, workers and others to protect and advance their interests.

A second criticism has focused on Braverman's argument that the de-skilling of white collar workers will lead to an increase in the working class. As Graeme Salaman argues, this neglects the important element of subjective identification of workers. This means that even de-skilled administrators and computer operators, for example, consider themselves – and therefore act and vote – as middle class.

BIBLIOGRAPHY

BRAVERMAN, H., *Labour and Monopoly Capitalism: the Degradation of Work in the Twentieth Century*, Monthly Review Press, 1974.
EDWARDS, R., *Contested Terrain: the Transformation of the Workplace in the Twentieth Century*, Heinemann, 1979.
SALAMAN, G., *Working*, Tavistock Publications, 1986.

Thomas J. Peters and Robert H. Waterman

Tom Peters and Bob Waterman had been partners in McKinsey and Company, the leading management consultancy firm, for many years when they undertook a study of excellence in American business. Their report, *In Search of Excellence*, became the most popular management book of recent years with up to 5 million copies sold worldwide. Peters now runs his own organization, founded to develop and propagate the ideas.

Peters and Waterman were concerned to examine and draw lessons from companies which were big (i.e. had annual turnovers of more than $1 billion) and which were well established (i.e. more than twenty years old). From the *Fortune 500* list of the largest US companies, forty-three companies were chosen which satisfied a number of performance criteria. They had to be of above average growth and financial return over a twenty-year period, plus having a reputation in their business sector for continuous innovation in response to changing markets. For all these firms, a full study of the published information on them over twenty-five years was carried out. In addition, about half the cases were the subject of extensive interview studies of the top managers involved; more limited interviews were conducted in the remaining half of the sample.

The companies designated to be excellent by this process include such leading names as Boeing, Hewlett-Packard, IBM, Johnson & Johnson, McDonald's, Proctor & Gamble and 3M. It is not claimed for these firms, and for the others classified as excellent, that they are without fault; they have made plenty of well-publicized mistakes. But overall they have performed well over long periods, and they are in a good position to continue as innovative in the future.

The interviews were concerned with top management organizing for success and how it is tackled in these excellent companies. Peters and Waterman soon decided that they could not stick to the formal aspects of managing: the organization chart, the budget plan, the balance sheet, the control graph. These highly analytical tools and concepts are inherently conservative. They lead to detailed forecasting and planning, and tight control: cost reduction becomes the priority and not revenue enhancement, for example. Above all, the philosophy behind the use of these narrowly rational techniques is to abhor mistakes, and therefore it does not value experimentation.

Such an approach cannot capture the distinctive nature of the excellent firms who innovate. A much wider range of processes must be considered. It must cover much that will be classified as informal, intuitive, irrational, intractable, but which cannot be ignored. Indeed it must be managed, as it has as much or more to do with the way companies excel (or fail), as do the formal structures and strategies.

Together with their colleagues Richard Pascale and Anthony Athos, Peters and Waterman developed a set of concepts to focus on what happens in the process of organizing, which became known as the McKinsey 7-S Framework. This is a series of seven interdependent aspects of organizing – all conveniently beginning with the letter 'S': structure, strategy, systems (and procedures), style (of management), skills (corporate strengths), staff (people) and shared values (culture). On the basis of this framework Peters and Waterman developed a set of eight attributes which characterize all excellent innovative US companies.

1. A BIAS FOR ACTION

Even though these companies may be analytical in their approach to decision-making, they are not paralysed by the analysis. They have a 'can do' and 'let's try' approach which favours experimentation. Managers do not rely on the formal information and control systems. They get out of their offices and keep in touch informally; 'MBWA – Management By Wandering Around', it is called at Hewlett-Packard. An open door policy at all levels is typical, as is the organizational fluidity which allows the setting up of small task forces (mainly of volunteers), with short deadlines, who are expected to come up with an answer to a problem *and then implement their proposals*.

2. CLOSE TO THE CUSTOMER

These companies offer good products because they do not regard the customer as a bloody nuisance, best ignored. They regularly listen to their customers, from whom they get some of their best product ideas. They have what amounts to an obsession about customer service. IBM, for example, trains its salesmen not to be salesmen but 'customer problem solvers'. Its claim to give the best customer service of any company in the world is backed up by a fleet of special assistants (including some of the best salesmen) who are on three-year secondments doing only one thing – dealing with every customer complaint within twenty-four hours.

3. AUTONOMY AND ENTREPRENEURSHIP

The innovative companies foster many leaders and many innovators throughout the organization. 3M, for example, is a hive of 'product champions', who have been allowed to be creative and who are feverishly trying to make their idea successful. Top management does not try to control so tightly that everyone feels stifled. They support practical risk-taking and they encourage internal competition. They have large numbers of innovations on the go and they can tolerate it when inevitably many fail – that is how they ensure that *some* succeed. The comparison with Burns's organic system of management (see p. 53) is very clear.

4. PRODUCTIVITY THROUGH PEOPLE

The excellent companies treat the ordinary members of the organization as the basic source of quality and productivity gains. They do not regard capital investment and labour substitution as the fundamental source of efficiency improvement. They strongly oppose an 'us–them' attitude in industrial relations and they treat workers as people. They are not soft; the people orientation has a tough side. They are very performance conscious, but the personal achievements stem from mutually high expectations and peer review rather than exhortation and complicated control systems.

McDonald's, for example, compare a well-run restaurant to a winning baseball team and always refer to workers as 'crew members'. They believe that senior managers should be out in the field paying attention to employees, to training, to the standard of service offered. They work hard to restrain and cut the corporate management, believing that the less there is, the better. Their commitment to productivity through people is illustrated by the 'McDonald's Hamburger University', out of which many crew members graduate, and the annual competition for the best 'All-American Hamburger Maker'.

5. HANDS-ON, VALUE DRIVEN

The basic philosophy of the excellent firms, the shared values of all the participants, may sound very 'soft' and abstract, but it has far more to do with their achievements than economic resources, technological developments, organizational structure or control systems. All of these factors have to change over the years but the philosophy must be established and maintained from the top to bottom of the firm. Those at the top work hard to maintain the values in a very public hands-on way. Their chief executives are famed throughout the company for getting involved in the actual processes (design, selling, etc.) thus publicly demonstrating their commitment to high standards.

This explicit understanding of, and commitment to, a system of values is probably the single most important key to excellence. Less successful firms either do not know what their values are, or have a set of objectives, but seem only to get fired up about quantitative ones (e.g. earnings per share, growth measures). These can motivate the top ten, fifty, even the top hundred managers, but larger firms need to propagate clear values throughout the whole organization. The content of the dominant beliefs is narrow in scope, but exhibited by all the firms. It includes a belief in being the best producer (whether the product is an aircraft, a hamburger or an advertising campaign) and in giving superior quality and service. The importance of the nuts and bolts of doing the job well, of informal methods of improving communication to achieve goals, of economic growth and profits, also feature strongly.

6. STICK TO THE KNITTING

Excellent companies do not wish to become conglomerates. 'Never acquire a business you don't know how to run' was how a retiring chairman of Johnson & Johnson put it to his successor. They have seen the way corporations like ITT have suffered through trying to spread into new business sectors by large acquisition. Excellent companies move out mainly through internally generated diversification, one manageable step at a time.

7. SIMPLE FORM, LEAN STAFF

As big as these companies are, the underlying structural forms and systems are elegantly simple. Top level staffs are lean: corporate staffs of fewer than a hundred people running multi-billion-dollar enterprises. Complicated structures which blur the lines of authority, such as matrix organization, are eschewed. The straightforward divisional form with the product divisions having all the functions of a business is used. The hiving off of successful new products into separate divisions is encouraged and rewarded at surprisingly small volumes (e.g. at about $20 m. turnover at 3M).

8. SIMULTANEOUS LOOSE–TIGHT PROPERTIES

The excellent companies are both centralized and decentralized. For the most part they have pushed autonomy downwards, to the division, to the product-development team, to the shop floor. On the other hand they are fanatical centralists around the few core values they see as key to the enterprise: quality, reliability, action, regular informal communication, quick feedback. These are ways of exerting extremely tight control and ensuring that nothing gets very far out of line. The attention to the customer is one of the tightest properties of all – not through massive forms and large numbers of control variables but through self and peer discipline making this the focus of activity. Thus the 'soft' concept of a philosophical value is, in fact, harder in its impact than setting target ratios in a control system. As one chief executive said: 'It's easy to fool the boss, but you can't fool your peers.'

These findings, Peters and Waterman underline, show that the excellent companies were, above all, 'brilliant on the basics'. They do not let techniques substitute for thinking nor analysis impede action. They work hard to keep things simple in a complex world. They tolerate some chaos in return for quick action and regular innovation. They prize their values as their most essential asset.

One conclusion that Peters and Waterman came to, rather reluctantly, was that associated with almost every excellent company was a strong leader who was instrumental in forming the culture of excellence in the early stages of the firm's development. Even so, they strongly believe that firms can change towards excellence.

Yet Peters starts a later book, *Thriving on Chaos*, with the statement: 'There are no excellent companies!' This is because the business world is changing so fast that no company is safe, not even those earlier designated as excellent, many of which have been in difficulties. All firms must continue to face up to the need for a revolution in organizations by emphasizing a new set of basic aims. These are enhanced responsiveness through greatly increased flexibility and continuous short-cycle innovation aimed at creating new markets for both new and mature products of world-class quality and service.

To help in achieving the necessary changes, Peters proposes forty-five specific prescriptions across five major business areas (customer responsiveness, fast-paced innovation, flexibility by empowering people, loving change and building new systems). For example, one of the ten prescriptions for 'creating total customer responsiveness' is 'be an internationalist'. Even small firms must early on look for business opportunities abroad: selling, designing, manufacturing. A prescription under learning to love change is 'create a sense of urgency', and one for building systems for a world turned upside-down is 'revamp the chief control tools'.

These aims may sound a tall order, but firms have no choice but to change and innovate in order to survive. If managers doubt this, they should look at what their fastest growing competitors are doing and see the writing on the wall.

BIBLIOGRAPHY

PETERS, T. J., and WATERMAN, R. H., *In Search of Excellence: Lessons from America's Best-Run Companies*, Harper & Row, 1982.

PETERS, T. J., *Thriving on Chaos: A Handbook of Management Revolution*, Macmillan, 1988.

PETERS, T. J., *The Pursuit of WOW*, Macmillan, 1994.

PETERS, T. J., *The Tom Peters Seminar*, Vintage Books, 1994.

Rosabeth Moss Kanter

Rosabeth Moss Kanter is a Professor of Business Administration at the Harvard Business School and a consultant to many organizations. A sociologist working in the tradition of Max Weber (see p. 5), she has carried out a historical study of American work communes. She has been the recipient of a Guggenheim Fellowship, and a McKinsey Award for a 1979 article in the *Harvard Business Review* on 'Power Failure in Management Circuits'. Her detailed study of the human aspects of the functioning of a major present-day US manufacturing company, *Men and Women of the Corporation*, was the 1977 winner of the C. Wright Mills award for the best book on social issues.

The study focused on three key roles in the company (code-named the Industrial Supply Corporation – 'Indsco'): those of managers, secretaries and wives. The managers, with a small minority of exceptions, were men; the secretaries and the wives were women, and Kanter's work analyses their relationships. It might seem strange to consider wives as part of the corporation, but in fact (although not in theory) this is how they were defined and treated. On the other hand, the husbands of the, relatively rare, female managers were not put in this position, being considered to be independent of Indsco.

Managers, particularly as they rise to the top, are required to cope with increasing uncertainty. Greater routinization applies primarily to the lower levels; managers have to be allowed to exercise discretion. They are therefore the recipients of the owners' and main Board's trust. At Indsco, the top managers inevitably chose people like themselves in whom to put this trust. The managers spent a lot of time interacting with each other – between a third and a half of their time actually in meetings. Interacting with people like yourself is always easier, and there was a decided wish to avoid those with whom communication was felt to be uncomfortable. Deviants and non-conformists were suspect; those who dressed differently raised questions because of the messages they might be conveying. Predictability had the highest value. It was acceptable to be somewhat contro-versial, as long as the manager was consistent and fitted in with the basic values of hard work (staying late at the office if necessary or taking work home) and loyalty (being committed to a long-term career with the company).

The response to the uncertainties of performance and the need for easy communication are great pressures for management to become a closed circle. Homogeneity is the prime criterion for selection, and social con-formity a standard for conduct. Women were clearly put in the category of the incomprehensible and unpredictable and, with rare exceptions, were excluded. Many managers reported that they felt uncomfortable in dealing with them. 'It took more time', 'They changed their minds all the time', 'I'm always making assumptions that turn out to be wrong', were typical comments. Some managers were prepared to admit that this was really saying something about themselves, but this then became another example of their preference for dealing with their own kind.

The secretary had a very distinctive role in the corporation. She has been defined as the 'office wife'. This is a revealing analogy because the term 'wife' denotes a traditional, not a bureaucratic relationship (using Weber's terms, see p. 6). The secretarial promotion ladder (a bureaucratic component of the role) was very short; most women got there before the age of thirty and were then stuck. The only way forward was a promotion in the status of her boss. This determined both the formal rank and the actual power of the secretary: the tasks remained more or less the same at all levels.

The secretary, therefore, had to live her organizational life through her boss. In Weber's terms this is the patrimonial traditional pattern, even though it is embedded in a formal bureaucratic system. Very untypically in a bureaucracy where people normally work with those just above and just below themselves in status and salary, the boss–secretary relationship allows two people working closely together to have very wide discrepan-cies in remuneration. The relationship encourages considerable depend-ency, and secretaries are expected to show loyalty and devotion to their bosses. They are expected to value non-material rewards such as prestige, personal feelings of being wanted and 'loved', and having a salary rather than wages (even though that salary may be less than many wages).

Although the corporate wife had no official employment relationship with Indsco, she still had a clear career progression. There were three phases, each with its own problems. The first was the technical phase, corresponding to the husband's specialist or early managerial job. At that stage he is engaged in a job, extremely demanding of time and energy, in which she can play no part. Conversely, he is under-involved at home, and she tends to leave him out of the activities there. This mutual exclusion is the major strain and resentment.

The second, managerial phase of the wife's career came when the husband entered middle and upper management and she was expected to perform social and hostess duties. At this stage her behaviour, her social adequacy, has a considerable bearing on the progress of her husband's career. Friendships are no longer just a personal matter but have business implications – as, for example, when an old friendship between two of the managers and their wives had to be dropped because one manager now far outranked the other. Gossip is important, and every wife is faced with the problem as to how far she is going to let her true feelings determine her social life, and how far to let her relationships be determined by company 'political' considerations.

The third career phase was the institutional one, with the husband at the top of the organization or in a position where he must represent it to the outside. Here the issue for both husband and wife is the public nature of almost all their activities. What for others would be defined as pleasure (playing golf, attending a symphony concert, giving a party) are part of the business, and indeed allowable for tax as a business expense. Charitable and community service activities, where the wife's role is especially prominent, may generate useful business. The corporation and its needs and relationships pervades the couple's whole life. Yet, because so much of the top manager's work is concerned with evaluating and being evaluated on personal grounds of trust and integrity, the wife is faced with the task of carrying out these activities as though they were highly personal, not ritualistic and contrived. Her job is to contribute to the image of her husband as a whole real man. Top wives have also to suppress their private beliefs, and one wife, for example, told how proud she was that she never at any time during her husband's career unburdened herself of her private views to anyone.

From her study of Indsco, Kanter sees three important general needs for change in the modern industrial corporation: improving the quality of working life (to stem the steady decrease in the numbers of those who say that their jobs are satisfying), creating equal employment opportunities for women and minorities, and opening opportunities for releasing aspirations for employees to make better use of their talents in contributing to the corporation. To achieve these objectives, changes in organization structures are needed.

One way to enhance opportunities would be to open the circle of management to promotion from a wider range of personnel (e.g. women, clerical workers). This should be based on their appraised competences to do such jobs, and ignore the segregated and restricted career paths which trap them into lower-level jobs. Changes would be required in the appraisal, promotion and career systems and in the design of jobs. Ways need to be found to create intermediate jobs which would act as career bridges into management.

Then empowering strategies, concerned with flattening the hierarchy, decentralization and creating autonomous work groups, are necessary Number-balancing strategies would aim to raise the proportion of women and other minorities in higher jobs. It is important to combat tokenism by ensuring that several such group members, not just a single representative, are hired and later promoted at the same time. All these strategies for change are required if 'affirmative action' policies are to be effective.

But Kanter is well aware of the difficulties in getting change in large corporations and this led her on to a study of 'change masters' – corporate entrepreneurs who are capable of anticipating the need for, and of leading, productive change. She carried out an in-depth study of ten major companies, each with a well-known reputation for progressive human-resource policies. The companies included General Electric, General Motors, Honeywell, Polaroid and Wang Laboratories.

By examining in detail 115 innovations and the factors which encouraged them, Kanter found a crucial distinction between organizations which can and do innovate, and those whose style of thought is against change and prevents innovation. Innovative firms have an 'integrative' approach to problems. They have a willingness to see problems as wholes and in their solutions to move beyond received wisdom, to challenge established practices. Entrepreneurial organizations are willing to operate at the edges of their competence, dealing with what they do not yet know (e.g. new investments, new markets, new products). They do not measure themselves by the standards of the past, but by their visions of the future.

They contrast very strongly with firms with a 'segmentalist' approach.

These see problems as narrowly as possible, independently of their context. Companies like this are likely to have segmented structures: a large number of compartments strongly walled off from one another – production department from marketing department, corporate managers from divisional managers, management from labour, men from women. As soon as a problem is identified, it is broken up and the parts dealt with by the appropriate departments. Little or no effort is given to the problem as an integrated whole. As a segmentalist manager, you are not going to start dealing with others' aspects of the problem and you would regard it as a personal failure if they were to start worrying about yours. So entrepreneurial spirit is stifled and the solution is unlikely to be innovative. It will follow the solid structure laid down. (This analysis is comparable to the organic versus mechanistic distinction of Burns, see p. 53.)

In describing cases of integrative organizations where innovations thrive, Kanter suggests a number of important elements necessary to reduce the segmentalism apparent in so many non-innovative, older, troubled firms. The aim is to reawaken the spirit of enterprise and arouse the potential entrepreneurs that exist in all organizations. The methods include encouragement of a culture of pride in the firm's own achievements, reduction of layers in the hierarchy, improvement of *lateral* communication, and giving of increased information about company plans. Decentralization is very important; as is the empowerment of entrepreneurial people lower down the organization to have the authority and the resources to exploit their ideas – even if this means cutting across established segments and boundaries.

In later books Kanter elaborates the need for organizations to change in order to be successful. They have to employ the four 'F's: being focused, fast, friendly and flexible. The *focused* aspect means developing internal synergies in leaner, more integrated organizations. This involves encouraging cooperative efforts in a less diversified business that can apply one unit's competence to another's problems. They should also be *fast* in actively promoting 'newstreams', i.e. creating official channels to speed the flow of new business possibilities within the firm. Thus the opportunities for innovation extend well beyond the R & D department, and many more people at more levels should be given the chance to lead new projects, encouraging 'interpreneurship'. *Friendly* companies find it easier to establish working alliances with other organizations. This allows them to extend their range without increasing in size. It gives them information access, windows on technology, speed of action and mutual accommodation to innovation. *Flexible* organizations have given up bureaucracy and reduced hierarchy, and work flexibly with a smaller fixed core of employees and a larger number of partnership ties.

This all adds up to a new approach of *post-entrepreneurial management* based on three principles:

1. Minimize obligations and maximize options. Keep fixed costs low and use variable means to achieve goals.
2. Derive power through influence and alliances rather than through full control or total ownership.
3. Keep things moving by encouraging continuous regrouping of people, functions and products to produce innovative combinations.

Only in this way will corporations learn to thrive in the global economy.

BIBLIOGRAPHY

KANTER, R. M., *Men and Women of the Corporation*, Basic Books, 1977.

KANTER, R. M., 'Power Failure in Management Circuits', *Harvard Business Review* (July–August 1979), 65–75; reprinted in D. S. Pugh (ed.), *Organization Theory*, Penguin, 1997.

KANTER, R. M., *The Change Masters: Corporate Entrepreneurs at Work*, Allen & Unwin, 1984.

KANTER, R. M., *When Giants Learn to Dance*, Simon & Schuster, 1989.

KANTER, R. M., *World Class*, Simon & Schuster, 1995.

Karl E. Weick

Karl Weick's lively view of managing and of organizing, active words which he prefers to the more static words 'management' and 'organization', matches the liveliness of his personal interests, which he says range from jazz big-bands to 'railroading'. In its essentials, his is the view of an American psychologist who has used his discipline imaginatively to deepen the understanding of this field of endeavour. Weick is Rensis Likert Collegiate Professor of Organizational Behaviour and Psychology at the University of Michigan.

As he sees organizations, they are 'sensemaking systems', which incessantly create and re-create conceptions of themselves and of all around them that seem sensible and stable enough to be manageable. Their members continually reaffirm to one another the truths of this reality as they see it, and the correctness of what should be done about it. Sensemaking is more than interpretation. It includes generating what is interpreted. People build up a view of themselves and what is going on, and at the same time interpret what was their own view in the first place. As Weick frequently puts it, 'people know what they think when they see what they say.'

So sensemaking is rolling hindsight. It is a continual weaving of sense from beliefs, from implicit assumptions, from tales from the past, from unspoken premises for decision and action, and from ideas about what will happen as a result of what can be done. Once put into words it is constrained and framed by those same words because they are only approximately what they refer to. Often words have multiple meanings, so all the time people are working with puns. Further, words are inclined to convey discrete categories: they are not equal to depicting the unbroken, complex flow of life in organizations.

The sense that is made is shaped also by selective perception, that is, by noticing some things and not others. Commitments that have been made then have to be justified retrospectively. There is a constant process of putting together reasoned arguments and arguing about them, most obviously in meetings which have a value as sensemaking occasions. However, the sense that is made has its limits. People with time to spend on a problem at a meeting make sense of it in a way most understandable to themselves, so others become less able to follow what is afoot. Showing up at meetings therefore produces a situation that is manageable only by those who have been showing up.

The whole sensemaking process gives ostensible orderliness to what is going on, and has gone on. The development of a 'generic sensemaking', within which individuals differ yet sufficiently concur, maintains a sense of organization.

Organizational sensemaking has at least seven distinguishing characteristics. It is:

1. *Grounded in identity construction*, for sensemakers perpetually redefine their notion of themselves.
2. *Retrospective*, a never-ending reconstruction of experience. We are in the position of explorers who never know what they are exploring until it has been explored.
3. *Enactive of sensible environments*, because people make sense of their worlds. By doing so they create, or enact, a part of the very environment they face. They implant their own reality. So an organization imposes on the environment that imposes on it, and the bigger it becomes the more it runs into what it has itself enacted. A manufacturer which defines itself as the monopoly supplier of a product will by that enactment hamper itself from perceiving that innovative subsitutes are a threat to its market. Most firms in the Swiss traditional watch industry, for example, just did not enact their environment to include cheap digital watches, and so suffered.
4. *Social*, since it occurs with and in relation to other people inside and outside the organization.
5. *Ongoing*, as it never stops and therefore never starts. Sensemaking is always in process.
6. *Focused on and by extracted cues*, that is, growing from familiar points of reference. Controlling these cues is a source of power, since controlling what others respond to frames the view they will take and what they will do.
7. *Driven by plausibility rather than accuracy*, for 'the sensible need not be

sensable.' People go along with what to them is plausible and credible even if it cannot be checked. It might also have some accuracy, but since an equivocal and changing world has always moved on before a precise account of it can be formulated, absolute accuracy is impossible. Hence accuracy takes second place to acceptability, to a version good enough to guide action for the time being.

Weick makes use of a published study on the knitwear industry in Scotland to illustrate these points. A number of small manufacturers in and around one town make cashmere sweaters. The managers of each see their own firms as having a distinct *identity*, signified by colour and design of product, within an industry having a collective high-quality identity that distinguishes it from other makers of sweaters. The industry claims to have a business strategy centred on a specific high-income market, a strategy which has developed *retrospectively* from experience of sales rather than one which has been planned with foresight. The sales agents whom the firms employ sell classically designed clothes, and therefore feed back information from that particular market which confirms the prior beliefs that the makers hold about it. Thus the latter constantly *re-enact* their environment, affirming this by *social* (including sociable) contacts in and between firms, the whole a continual *ongoing* process during which *cues* from designers, trade shows and shops, as well as from the agents, reinforce the particular way in which the situation is perceived and so sustain its *plausibility*.

This is a long-established industry where sensemaking is moulded by hand-craft traditions. In younger organizations with professionally qualified employees, sensemaking has freer range, especially when innovative, non-routine decisions are to be made. Here the enactment of environments and the self-fulfilling prophecies that result from this should be most conspicuous. If, however, these newer organizations follow the current fashion and set up self-managed teams, their sensemaking will become less generic and more fragmented. Each team will make sense of things in its own way.

Excellent illustrations of the impact of the enacted nature of organizational sensemaking are given by an examination of crisis situations. These are so complex that the enactments of the individuals involved will inevitably be partial, and their interactions may well exacerbate the crisis. Weick uses the example of the industrial disaster at the Union Carbide plant in Bhophal, India, to show how it was the preconceptions of everybody involved, from senior managers to operators, that determined which action was taken. Their enacted views of their situation led to disaster. He wryly quotes the operating manual. After telling operators to dump the gas into a spare tank if a leak cannot be stopped, this reads: 'There may be other situations not covered above. The situation will determine the appropriate action.' In fact, it was the other way round: the actions of the managers and operators determined the disaster situation. For example, after early safety violations had been corrected, top management regarded the plant as 'safe'. This preconception allowed them to undertake methods of reducing the operating costs of 'a safe plant' in ways which, in the event, contributed to the disaster. Again, the operators had long dismissed an operating gauge as dysfunctional, having had trouble with it. They therefore neglected its correct reading in the disaster situation – a blind spot which had an important bearing on their attempts to make sense of what was happening. This is not to blame them; we often cannot know what 'the appropriate action' should be until we are involved in doing something, seeing what happens and making sense of it.

Paradoxically, if sensemaking constructs relatively stable interpretations, then this would render a flexible organic form of organization (see Burns, p. 53) steadily less so, and steadily less effective if it continued to be in an instable environment. This might account for the tendency of organic organizations to drift towards the mechanistic form.

Whatever the form of organization, some of its elements will be tightly coupled together whilst the coupling of others will be comparatively loose. Weick derives the concept of *loose coupling* from work by March (see p. 137) and others. It means that if some of the parts or activities in an organization change, the effect of this on other parts or activities will be limited, or be slow to show, or both. The mutual influence of loosely coupled systems is low.

Loose coupling facilitates adaptation. In a loosely coupled organization there can be differential change, some aspects changing faster or more than others, so that overall there is a flexible response by the organization. Because bonds *within* loosely coupled sub-assemblies are stronger than those *between* them (for example, within work groups or departments as against between work groups or departments), there is both stability and flexibility.

Whatever the form of organization, it will have to work with ambiguous, uncertain, equivocal and changing information. Despite their façade of numbers and objectivity and accountability, organizations and those who manage them wade amidst guesswork, subjectivity and arbitrariness. Weick feels that language could better reflect this constant ambiguous flux by making more use of verbs and less of nouns. Indeed, he urges people to 'stamp out nouns': to think of managing rather than management, of organizing rather than organization, as noted earlier.

He offers managers and others in organizations ten further 'pieces of advice':

1. *Don't panic in the face of disorder.* Some degree of disorder is necessary so that disorderly, ambiguous information can be taken in and coped with, rather than tidily screened out.

2. *You never do one thing all at once.* Whatever you do has many ramifications, not just the one you have in mind. And whilst some consequences happen right away, others show up indirectly and much later.

3. *Chaotic action is preferable to orderly inaction.* When someone asks 'What shall I do?' and is told 'I don't know, just do something', that is probably good advice. Since sense is made of events retrospectively, an action, any action, provides something to make sense of. Inaction is more senseless.

4. *The most important decisions are often the least apparent.* Decisions about what is to be retained in files, in databases, in memories indeed, provide the basis for future action. Such decisions may not be conspicuous, yet they sustain the past from which the future is begun.

5. *There is no solution.* As there are no simple answers, and rarely is anything right or wrong, learn to live with improvisation and just a tolerable level of reasonableness.

6. *Stamp out utility.* Good adaptation now rules out some options for the future. Concentrating overmuch on utility now can rule out sources of future utility. Resources and choices are used up. Better to retain some noise and variability in the system, even at a cost to present efficiency, so that fresh future repertoires of action may be opened up.

7. *The map is the territory.* When the managers' map of what causes what, drawn from past experience, is superimposed on the future, it becomes for them the territory that it maps. Simplification though it is, such a map has been worked over more than any other product has, and is as good a guide as can be had.

8. *Rechart the organizational chart.* Do not be boxed in by its conventional form. See things as they work out and people as they are to you. See the chart in the way that it functions. For example, in the box on the chart for chairman write 'hesitancy'; in the box for general manager write 'assertiveness', and so on, in the way people come over to you.

9. *Visualize organizations as evolutionary systems.* See what is evolving, and what you can and should change. Likewise, recognize what is not, and you cannot.

10. *Complicate yourself!* Consider different causes, other solutions, new situations, more complex alternatives, and take pleasure in the process of doing so.

Weick does his best to follow his own tenth piece of advice and to always move on, towards other ways of looking at organizing and organizers.

BIBLIOGRAPHY

WEICK, K. E., *The Social Psychology of Organizing*, Addison-Wesley, 1969, 2nd ed., 1979.

WEICK, K. E., *Sensemaking in Organizations*, Sage, 1995.

WEICK, K. E., 'Enacted sensemaking in crisis situations', *Journal of Management Studies*, 25, 1988, 305–17; reprinted in D. S. Pugh (ed.), *Organization Theory*, Penguin, 1997.

FOUR

Decision-Making in Organizations

The task of administration is so to design this environment that the individual will approach as close as practicable to rationality (judged in terms of the organization's goals) in his decisions.

HERBERT A. SIMON

An organization is a collection of choices looking for problems, issues and feelings looking for decision situations in which they might be aired, solutions looking for issues to which they might be the answers, and decision-makers looking for work.

JAMES G. MARCH

It makes more sense to talk about participative and autocratic situations than it does to talk about participative and autocratic managers.

VICTOR H. VROOM

An organization can be considered as a set of games between groups of partners who have to play with each other.

MICHEL CROZIER

Although writers have considered a range of aspects of organizational functioning, there has been a continuing school of thought which maintains that it is the analysis of decision-making which is the key to understanding organizational management processes.

This approach was inaugurated by Herbert Simon and his colleagues of Carnegie-Mellon University. For Simon, management is decision-making. His colleague James March develops this approach to consider the non-rationality of decision processes.

Victor Vroom proposes a theory of appropriate decision-making styles, and Michel Crozier examines the nature of the power which is at the basis of the decision-making 'game'.

Herbert A. Simon

Herbert Simon is a distinguished American political and social scientist whose perceptive contributions have influenced thinking and practice in many fields. He began his career in public administration and operations research, but as he took appointments in successive universities his interests encompassed all aspects of administration. He is Professor of Computer Science and Psychology at Carnegie Mellon University, Pittsburgh, where he and his colleagues have been engaged on fundamental research into the processes of decision-making, using computers to simulate human thinking. Herbert Simon's outstanding intellectual contribution was publicly recognized when, in 1978, he was awarded the Nobel Prize for Economics.

For Simon 'management' is equivalent to 'decision-making' and his major interest has been an analysis of how decisions are made and of how they might be made more effectively.

He describes three stages in the overall process of making a decision:

1. Finding occasions calling for a decision – the *intelligence* activity (using the word in the military sense).
2. Inventing, developing and analysing possible courses of action – the *design* activity.
3. Selecting a particular course of action from those available – the *choice* activity.

Generally speaking, intelligence activity precedes design, and design activity precedes choice; but the sequence of stages can be much more complex than this. Each stage in itself can be a complex decision-making process. The design stage can call for new intelligence activities. Problems at any stage can generate a series of sub-problems which in turn have their intelligence, design and choice stages. Nevertheless, in the process of organizational decision-making these three general stages can be discerned.

Carrying out the decisions is also regarded as a decision-making process.

Thus after a policy decision has been taken, the executive having to carry it out is faced with a wholly new set of problems involving decision-making. Executing policy amounts to making more detailed policy. Essentially, for Simon, all managerial action is decision-making.

On what basis do administrators make decisions? The traditional theory of economists assumed complete rationality. Their model was of 'economic man' (which, of course, embraced woman), who deals with the real world in all its complexity. He selects the rationally determined best course of action from among all those available to him in order to maximize his returns. But clearly this model is divorced from reality. We know that there is a large non-rational element in people's thinking and behaviour. The need for an administrative theory is precisely because there are practical limits to human rationality. These limits to rationality are not static but depend upon the organizational environment in which the individual's decision takes place. It then becomes the task of administration so to design this environment that the individual will approach as close as practicable to rationality in decisions, as judged in terms of the organization's goals.

In place of 'economic man' Simon proposes a model of 'administrative man'. While economic man maximizes (i.e. selects the best course from those available), administrative man 'satisfices' – looking for a course of action that is satisfactory or 'good enough'. In this process decision-makers are content with gross simplifications, taking into account only those comparatively few relevant factors which their minds can manage to encompass. 'Most human decision-making, whether individual or organizational, is concerned with the discovery and selection of satisfactory alternatives; only in exceptional cases is it concerned with the discovery and selection of optimal alternatives.' Most decisions are concerned not with searching for the sharpest needle in the haystack but with searching for a needle sharp enough to sew with. Thus administrators who 'satisfice' can make decisions without searching for all the possible alternatives and can use relatively simple rules of thumb. In business terms they do not look for 'maximum profit' but 'adequate profit'; not 'optimum price' but 'fair price'. This makes their world much simpler.

What techniques of decision-making are then available? In discussing this problem, Simon makes a distinction between two polar types of decisions: *programmed* and *non-programmed* decisions. These are not mutually exclusive but rather make up a continuum stretching from highly programmed decisions at one end to highly unprogrammed decisions at the other. Decisions are programmed to the extent that they are repetitive and routine or a definite procedure has been worked out to deal with them. They thus do not have to be considered afresh each time they occur. Examples would be the decisions involved in processing a customer's order, determining an employee's sickness benefit or carrying out any routine job.

Decisions are unprogrammed to the extent that they are new and unstructured or where there is no cut-and-dried method for handling the problem. This may be either because it has not occurred before, or because it is particularly difficult or important. Examples would be decisions to introduce a new product, make substantial staff redundancies or move to a new location. All these decisions would be non-programmed (although entailing many programmed sub-decisions) because the organization would have no detailed strategy to govern its responses to these situations, and it would have to fall back on whatever general capacity it had for intelligent problem-solving.

Human beings are capable of acting intelligently in many new or difficult situations but they are likely to be less efficient. The cost to the organization of relying on non-programmed decisions in areas where special-purpose procedures and programmes can be developed is likely to be high, and an organization should try to programme as many of its decisions as possible. The traditional techniques of programmed decision-making are habit, including knowledge and skills, clerical routines and standard operating procedures, and the organization's structure and culture, i.e. its system of common expectations, well-defined information channels, established sub-goals, etc. The traditional techniques for dealing with non-programmed decisions rely on the selection and training of executives who possess judgement, intuition and creativity. These categories of technique have been developed over thousands of years (the building of the pyramids must have involved the use of many of them). But since the Second World War, Simon argues, a complete revolution in techniques of decision-making has got under way, comparable to the invention of powered machinery in manufacture.

This revolution has been due to the application of such techniques as mathematical analysis, operational research, electronic data processing, information technology and computer simulation. These were used first for completely programmed operations (e.g. mathematical calculations, accounting procedures) formerly regarded as the province of clerks. But more and more elements of judgement (previously unprogrammed and the province of middle management) can now be incorporated into programmed procedures. Decisions on stock control and production control have been in the forefront of this development. With advances in computer technology, more and more complex decisions will become programmed. Even a completely unprogrammed decision, made once and for all, can be reached via computer techniques by building a model of the decision situation. Various courses of action can then be simulated and their effects assessed. 'The automated factory of the future,' Simon maintains, 'will operate on the basis of programmed decisions produced in the automated office beside it.'

BIBLIOGRAPHY

SIMON, H. A., *Administrative Behaviour*, 2nd edn, Macmillan, 1960.

SIMON, H. A., *The New Science of Management Decision*, Harper & Row, 1960.

SIMON, H. A., *The Shape of Automation*, Harper & Row, 1965.

MARCH, J. G., and SIMON, H. A., *Organizations*, Wiley, 1958.

James G. March

James March is Professor of Management at Stanford University, California. His breadth of mind is indicated by his being linked also with the departments of Political Science and of Sociology. His interests have long focused upon decision-making in organizations, ever since his early work at Carnegie-Mellon University. Its renowned contributors to the understanding of decision-making include also Herbert Simon (see p. 133) and Richard Cyert, both colleagues of March and both still at Carnegie-Mellon, Cyert for many years as its President.

March himself brings to his lively analyses of decision-making a unique blend of the logical and the poetical. His work is logical in argument, poetical in imagery and expression. He feels that decision-making can be understood in much the same non-rational way as a painting by Picasso or a poem by T. S. Eliot. It is far from a rationally controlled process moving steadily to a culminating choice. The confusion and complexity surrounding decision-making is underestimated. Many things are happening at once. Views and aims are changing, and so are alliances between those concerned. What has to be done is not clear, nor is how to do it. In this topsy-turvy world where people do not comprehend what is going on, decisions may have little to do with the processes that supposedly make them, and organizations 'do not know what they are doing'.

It is a world in which there are cognitive, political, and organizational limits to rationality. Cognitively, attention is the key scarce resource. Individuals cannot attend to everything at once, nor can they be everywhere at once. So they attend to some parts of some decision-making, not to all of it. What they attend to depends upon the alternative claims upon them, since giving attention to one decision means overlooking others. As March puts it, 'every entrance is an exit somewhere else'. Therefore timing is crucial, timing when to join in and which matters to raise.

March shares with his former colleague Simon the conception of *bounded* rationality. Not only is attention scarce; mental capacity is limited. The mind of the decision-maker can only encompass so much. It can only cope with a limited amount of information, and with a limited number of alternatives. That being so, even if decision-making is intended to be rational, there are severe bounds to its rationality. Decisions will be taken knowing much less than in principle could be known.

Along with scarce attention and bounded rationality come erratic preferences. People change their minds as to what they want. Even if they know what they want, they may ignore their own preferences and follow other advice or other traditions. They may state their preferences in an ambiguous way. Their preference may conflict with the preferences of others.

Here the cognitive limits to rationality connect with the political limits. March and his other former colleague Cyert recognize that a firm, and indeed any other kind of organization, is a shifting multiple-goal political coalition. 'The composition of the firm is not given; it is negotiated. The goals of the firm are not given; they are bargained.' The coalition, to use their word, includes managers, workers, stockholders, suppliers, customers, lawyers, tax collectors and other agents of the state, as well as all the sub-units or departments into which an organization is divided. Each have their own preferences about what the firm should be like and what its goals should be. Hence negotiation and bargaining rather than detached rationality are endemic.

This is where the political limits to rationality connect with the organizational limits. These are the limits set by *organized anarchies*. Though organizations do not have the properties of organized anarchy all of the time, they do for part of the time, and especially if they are publicly owned or are educational, such as universities, colleges and schools. Organized anarchies have 'three general properties'. First, since preferences are unclear, the organization discovers its goals from what it is doing rather than by defining them clearly in advance. Second, since it has 'unclear technology', 'its own processes are not understood by its members' and it works by trial and error more than by knowing what it is doing. Third, since there is 'fluid participation', who is involved in what is constantly changing. Take a college, for instance. Pronouncements on strategy are more reviews of what courses are already taught than they are statements of future goals; new teaching techniques such as video games are tried without knowing whether they will work and without their being understood by authorizing committees; and what such committees understand and approve depends on who turns up to meetings.

Given these cognitive, political and organizational characteristics, decision-making processes are bound to be affected. Not only in those organizations prone to organized anarchy, but even in business firms such decision processes have four peculiarities. They are:

1. Quasi-resolution of conflict
2. Uncertainty avoidance
3. Problemistic search
4. Organizational learning

Quasi-resolution of conflict is the state of affairs most of the time. The conflicts inherent in the political nature of organizations and therefore in the making of decisions are not resolved. Rather there are devices for their quasi-resolution which enable them to be lived with. One such device is 'local rationality'. Since each sub-unit or department deals only with a narrow range of problems – the sales department with 'how to sell' and the personnel department with 'how to recruit' and so on – each can at least purport to be rational in dealing with its 'local' concerns. Of course, these local rationalities can be mutually inconsistent (as when accounting's insistence on remaining within budget destroys marketing's advertising campaign), so they may not add up to overall rationality for the organization as a whole.

A second such device can ease this difficulty. It is 'acceptable level decision rules'. The acceptable level of consistency between one decision and another is low enough for the divergences to be tolerable. What is needed is an outcome acceptable to the different interests rather than one that is optimal overall. Third, 'sequential attention to goals' also helps. As the conflicts between goals are not resolved, attention is given first to one goal and then to another in sequence. For example, smooth production is first emphasized, then later on the priority switches to satisfying customers by design variations which disrupt production.

Uncertainty avoidance, too, pervades decision-making. All organizations must live with uncertainty. Customer orders are uncertain, so are currency fluctuations, so is future taxation, and so on. Therefore, decision-making responds to information here and now, and avoids the uncertainties of longer-term forecasting. Pressing problems are dealt with, and planning for the longer run is avoided. Market uncertainties are avoided by exclusive contracts with customers, and by conforming with everyone else to recognized pricing and negotiating practices. For the same reason *search is problemistic* and short-sighted. The occurrence of a problem spurs a search for ways to deal with it, and once a way is found then search stops. Far-sighted regular search, such as the steady accumulation of market information, is relatively unimportant. Such information is likely to be ignored in the urgency of any particular sales crisis. Moreover, search is 'simple-minded'. When a problem arises, search for a solution is concentrated near the old solution. Radical proposals are brushed aside and a safer answer is found not much different from what there was before. When an American university sought a new dean to head a major faculty, prominent outsiders were passed over and an established insider chosen because of fears that outsiders might make too many changes. Business organizations, too, regularly choose both managers and workers to fit in with the least disruption to existing set-ups.

Finally, decision-making processes are learning processes. In them, *organizational learning* takes place. Decision-makers do not begin by knowing all they need to know. They learn as they go. They learn what is thought practicable and what is not, what is permissible and what is not. By trial and error they find out what can be done and adapt their goals to it.

Perhaps it should not be surprising that all this leads March, together with Cohen and Olsen, to propose a *garbage can model of organizational choice*, famed for its name as well as for what it postulates. For when people fight for the right to participate in decision-making and then do not exercise it, when they request information and then do not use it, when they struggle over a decision and then take little interest in whether it is ever carried out, something curious must be going on.

So, the opportunity or the need to arrive at a decision, to make a choice, can be seen as 'a garbage can into which various kinds of problems and solutions are dumped by participants as they are generated'. There may be several garbage cans around with different labels on.

In the model so vividly depicted, a decision is an outcome of the interplay between *problems*, *solutions*, *participants* and *choices*, all of which arrive relatively independently one of another. Problems can arise inside or outside the organization. Solutions exist on their own irrespective of problems (people's preferences wait for their moment to come, the computer waits for the question it can answer). Participants move in and out. Opportunities for choices occur any time an organization is expected to produce a decision (e.g. when contracts must be signed or money must be spent).

The decisions come about by *resolution*, by *oversight* or by *flight*. If by resolution, then the choice resolves the problem, though this is likely to take time. If by oversight, the choice is made quickly, incidentally to other choices being made. If by flight, the original problem has gone (flown) away, leaving a choice which can now be readily made but solves nothing. Probably most decisions are made by oversight or flight, not by resolution.

Whether or not a decision happens is due to the 'temporal proximity' of what streams into the garbage can. That is, a decision happens when suitable problems, solutions, participants and choices coincide. When they do, solutions are attached to problems and problems to choices by participants who happen to have the time and energy to do it. So the decision that is made may be more or less 'uncoupled' from the apparent process of making it, being due to other coincidental reasons.

Seen like this, 'an organization is a collection of choices looking for problems, issues and feelings looking for decision situations in which they might be aired, solutions looking for issues to which they might be the answer, and decision-makers looking for work.' Though this may be so anywhere, nowhere is it more so than in an organized anarchy such as a university.

March admits that the picture may be overdrawn, but contends it is real enough to mean that the rational 'technology of reason' should be supplemented with a 'technology of foolishness'. Sometimes people *should* act *before* they think, so that they may discover new goals in the course of that action. They *should* make decisions with consequences for the future, in the knowledge that they do not know what will be wanted in the future. In terms of ostensible rationality, this is foolish. But decision-making needs scope for foolishness. Playfulness allows this. Playfulness is a deliberate (but temporary) suspension of the normal rational rules so that we can experiment. We need to play with foolish alternatives and *in*consistent possibilities. We need to treat goals as hypotheses to be changed, intuitions as real, hypocrisy as a transitional inconsistency, memory as an enemy of novelty and experience not as fixed history but as a theory of what happened, but which we can change if that helps us to learn. From time to time we should be foolishly playful inside our garbage cans.

BIBLIOGRAPHY

MARCH, J. G., *Decisions and Organizations*, Blackwell, 1988.

MARCH, J. G., *A Primer on Decision-Making*, Free Press, 1994.

CYERT, R. M., and MARCH, J. G., *A Behavioural Theory of the Firm*, Prentice-Hall, 1963.

MARCH, J. G., and OLSEN, J. P., *Ambiguity and Choice in Organizations*, Universitetsforlaget (Bergen, Norway), 1976.

Victor H. Vroom

Victor Vroom has been involved for many years in research, teaching and consulting on the psychological analysis of behaviour in organizations. A Canadian by birth, he has been at McGill University, a number of US universities and is currently Searle Professor of Organization and Management, and Professor of Psychology at Yale University. His interest in the effects of personality and participation in decision making began early and his doctoral dissertation on this topic won him the Ford Foundation Doctoral Dissertation Competition in 1959. He has also won the McKinsey Foundation Research Design Competition and the J. M. Cattel award of the American Psychological Association.

Vroom's dissertation corroborated previous findings that participation in decision-making has positive effects on attitudes and motivation. But in addition it showed that the size of these effects was a function of certain personality characteristics of the participants. Authoritarians and persons with weak independence needs are unaffected by the opportunity to participate; whereas equalitarians and those with strong independence needs develop more positive attitudes and greater motivation for effective performance through participation. The study did point out that there are a number of different processes related to participation which might be affected differently.

Much more recently Vroom (in collaboration with P. W. Yetton and A. G. Jago) has explored in much greater depth the processes of management decision-making and the variations in subordinate participation which can come about. Possible decision processes which a manager might use in dealing with an issue affecting a group of subordinates are as follows (though there are some variations if the issue concerns one subordinate only):

AI You solve the problem or make the decision yourself, using information available to you at that time.

AII   You obtain the necessary information from your subordinate(s), then decide on the solution to the problem yourself. You may or may not tell your subordinates what the problem is when getting the information from them. The role played by your subordinates in making the decision is clearly one of providing necessary information to you, rather than generating or evaluating alternative solutions.

CI   You share the problem with relevant subordinates individually, getting their ideas and suggestions without bringing them together as a group. Then *you* make the decisions that may or may not reflect your subordinates' influence.

CII   You share the problem with your subordinates as a group, collectively obtaining their ideas and suggestions. Then *you* make the decision that may or may not reflect your subordinates' influence.

GII   You share the problem with your subordinates as a group. Together you generate and evaluate alternatives and attempt to reach agreement (consensus) on a solution. Your role is much like that of chairman. You do not try to influence the group to adopt 'your' solution and you are willing to accept and implement any solution that has the support of the entire group.

Processes AI and AII are designated autocratic processes, CI and CII consultative processes, and GII is a group process. (GI applies to single subordinate issues.) Having identified these processes Vroom and Yetton's research programme then proceeded to answer two basic questions:

1. What decision-making processes *should* managers use to deal effectively with the problems they encounter in their jobs? This is a normative or prescriptive question. To answer it would require setting up a logical 'model' with a series of steps or procedures by which managers could rationally determine which was the most effective process to inaugurate.
2. What decision-making processes *do* managers use in dealing with their problems and what factors affect their choice of processes and degree of subordinate participation? This is a descriptive question, and the answer is important in delineating how far away from a rational approach managers are in their decision-making. We could then ask what

activities of training or development could lead managers to a more effective decision–making style.

It is in their answer to the first question that Vroom and his collaborators have made a most distinctive contribution. They have developed a detailed normative model of decision–making processes based on rational principles consistent with existing evidence on the consequences of participation for organizational effectiveness. They begin by distinguishing three classes of consequences which influence decision effectiveness:

1. The quality or rationality of the decision – clearly a process which jeopardized this would be ineffective.
2. The acceptance or commitment on the part of the subordinates to execute the decision effectively – if this commitment is necessary then processes which do not generate it even though they give a high-quality decision would be ineffective.
3. The amount of time required to make the decision – a decision process which took less time, if it were equally effective, would normally be preferable to one which took longer.

These consequences generate a set of rules for the model which may then be applied to the characteristics of a manager's problem under consideration. The model will then indicate which of the decision processes is appropriate to the particular case. The model can be expressed in the form of a decision tree, as shown on page 146. In the Decision Model, the problem characteristics are presented as questions. The manager starts at the left-hand side and moves to the right along the path determined by the answer to the question above each box. At the final point of the line the model shows which of the decision processes should be used to reach, in the least time, a quality decision which will be found acceptable.

As will be seen from the Decision Model, all decision processes (autocratic, consultative, group) are applicable in some circumstances and how often each should be used will depend on the type of decisions that the manager has to take. The normative model requires that all managers, if they are to be rational and effective, have to be able to operate across the whole range. In later work Vroom and Jago have elaborated the model to give greater discrimination among options and thus allow more detailed

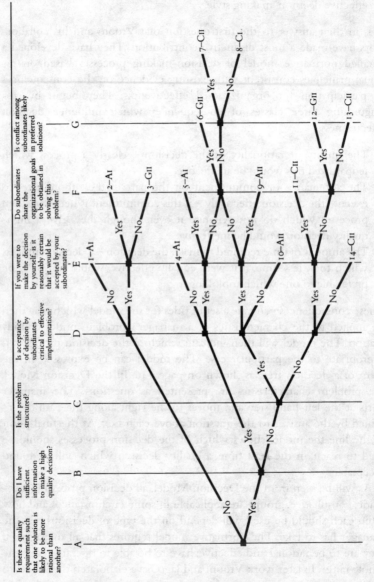

Decision Model (from Vroom and Yetton, 1973).

and more effective targeting of the decision process to the manager's problem. They have also made the more elaborate model available for use via a computer program.

The research undertaken by Vroom and his collaborators to answer their second question – how do managers actually behave? – is based on two methods. In the first, many managers were asked to recall decision problems and how they tackled them in terms of the questions of the Decision Model. The second method involved many managers assessing a set of standardized problem descriptions and giving their preferred solutions.

The most striking finding of these descriptive studies was that, while there were certainly average differences between managers in their use of various decision processes, these were small in comparison with the *range* of processes used by any individual manager. No managers indicated that they would use the same process on all decisions and most used all five of the decision processes above under some circumstances. 'It makes more sense to talk about participative and autocratic situations than it does to talk about participative and autocratic managers.'

The descriptive research also enabled a comparison of what managers do (or say they would do) and what the model would designate as rational behaviour. On average, a 'typical' manager was found to use the same decision process as that required by the Decision Model in 40 per cent of the situations. In a further quarter of the situations they used a process which is called 'feasible' in that it satisfied the constraints of the model on protecting decision quality and acceptability, but it would not be the least time-consuming. Only in about one third of the situations did the typical manager initiate a process which would risk quality or acceptability. In addition it was found that the constraints necessary to achieve acceptability were much more frequently ignored than those necessary to achieve quality.

Vroom has designed a leadership development programme based on his normative model which will enable managers to analyse their own decision processes against that of the model and see where they depart from the rational constraints for effective decision-making. The model proposes far greater variation for each problem situation than the typical manager exhibits. Using the model as a basis for making decisions would require such a manager to become both more autocratic *and* more participative according to the problem.

BIBLIOGRAPHY

VROOM, V. H., *Some Personality Determinants of the Effects of Participation*, Prentice-Hall, 1960.

VROOM, V. H., and YETTON, P. W., *Leadership and Decision-Making*, University of Pittsburgh Press, 1973.

VROOM, V. H., and JAGO, A. G., *The New Leadership: Managing Participation in Organizations*, Prentice-Hall, 1988.

Michel Crozier

The distinctly French view of organizations contributed by Michel Crozier arises both from his French birth and experience and from the many periods he has spent in the United States. These periods away from France give him a perspective on his own society. He has been Director of the Centre for the Sociology of Organizations in Paris, under the auspices of the Centre National de la Recherche Scientifique (CNRS), and has a long record of research in France. This has covered a wide range of organizations and administrative and social problems, but with an emphasis on studies of public administration and state-owned industries. However, his early training in sociology was in the United States, and he has spent many subsequent periods at Stanford and Harvard.

Although Crozier's view has its origins in research in France, it penetrates bureaucracies everywhere. He does not see them as monolithic rational structures, but as systems in which, despite all efforts at control, individuals and groups of individuals have room for manoeuvre. There is a constant interaction between the system and the actors in the system.

This view is distinctively founded on the concept of the power *game*. An organization is seen as a series of enmeshed power games, an 'ensemble' of games. This idea is no mere colourful image. Games are very real to those in organizations. Indeed, an organization is not so much the direct creation of deliberate design as the result of the ensemble of games. The game channels power relationships and enables cooperation, reconciling the freedom of those in the organization with the constraints it places upon them.

Games are played between groups of partners of many kinds, for example, between superiors and subordinates, such as managers and workers, or between departments and sections. The players evolve different strategies which govern what they do. Superiors may follow a strategy of 'divide and rule'; subordinates may follow a defensive strategy to protect whatever scope they may have to do things in their own way, free of interference from bosses or new regulations; occupational groups such as maintenance engineers may follow conservative (or aggressive) strategies toward technical modernization, and so on. Crozier calls this a *strategic model* of organization.

Players go so far but not too far in pursuing their strategies. While all are free to gain whatever advantage can be got from a strategy rationally designed to serve their interests, the continuance of the organization is necessary for them to be able to play at all. These are not life-and-death struggles but games for position within a system, therefore limits are accepted. These are the rules of the game which players in each game must respect if it is to continue. They are not formally set-down rules, but principles which can be discovered by analysing the players' recurrent behaviour, in the same way as their strategies can be seen in what they do. There may not be complete consensus on the rules, and some players may be endeavouring to change them, but they are sufficiently acknowledged and persistent for newcomers to learn them and to absorb the associated norms and values which define acceptable and unacceptable strategies.

The players in a game are far from equal – some are more powerful than others – and their roles differ further between games, so that players who are powerful in one game may be weak in another. However, their strategies share a common fundamental objective – to gain whatever advantage is possible, within the constraining rules of the game, by restricting the choices of alternatives open to others while preserving or enhancing their own choices. The aim is to manoeuvre others into positions where their actions can be determined, while retaining one's own freedom of action. All attempt to defend and extend their own discretion and to limit their dependence, while placing others in the reverse position.

The most revealing case among those described by Crozier is that of the maintenance workers in what he terms the 'Industrial Monopoly', the French nationalized tobacco industry. At the time of Crozier's research, at the end of the 1950s and beginning of the 1960s, this was dispersed throughout the country in a large number of small and very similar factories. Each employed in the order of 350 to 400 people of which perhaps one third were direct production workers. These workers were women, and their job was to operate the semi-automatic machines turning out cigarettes, etc.

The organization was very stable, and each small factory worked in a controlled environment. Finance, raw material procurement, distribution and sales were all centrally controlled from Paris, so each local plant could get on with its task of production, unimpeded by problems. Except one. Machine stoppages.

These stoppages occurred because of breakdowns and because of variations in the tobacco leaf which required constant adjustment of machines. They were the only major happenings that could not be dealt with by impersonal bureaucratic rules or bureaucratic actions from Paris. Yet if machines stopped, work stopped, and the factory stopped making what it was there for. Who could do something about it? Only the dozen or so male maintenance workers under the factory's technical engineer, who alone knew how to set and to repair the machines. No bureaucrat in Paris, no local factory director, not even the production workers on the machines, knew what they knew. They acquired the tricks of their trade from one another, and kept them to themselves. They did not explain what they did to anyone else. In their eyes it was an unforgivable sin for a production worker herself to 'fool around' with her machine, which she should not touch beyond operating it in the normal way. Thus the maintenance workers succeeded in making the production workers directly, and everyone else indirectly, dependent upon them. All the others were constrained by the maintenance workers being the only ones able to deal with stoppages, whilst the maintenance workers themselves preserved their freedom of choice over what to do.

They could do so because they were powerful; and they were powerful because of their 'control over the last source of uncertainty remaining in a completely routinized organizational system'. Machine stoppages occurred unpredictably and theirs was the choice of what to do. This gave them power because those who face and cope with uncertainties have power over others who are dependent upon their choices. In the long run, power is closely related to those uncertainties on which the life of an organization depends, and the strategies of the groups in the power games are aimed at controlling the 'ultimate strategic sources of uncertainties'. *Uncertainty explains power* (see also Hicks, p. 17).

The maintenance workers therefore had power because whilst everything else was under bureaucratic control the uncertain machine stoppages were not. These had to be dealt with on the spot as they happened. They presented the maintenance workers with an opportunity which was conspicuous because it was the sole uncertainty in each factory. In other organizations the sources of uncertainty may not be so conspicuous, but in all organizations they come and go and as they do so the power of those who confront them waxes and wanes. Maintenance workers are only one example: the same applies to the rise and fall of financial experts, of production control specialists, and so on.

Why is it then that powerful experts are not able to cling to power indefinitely? If the uncertainty continues and with it their know-how they could indeed keep their grip on power, but this is unlikely because their success is self-defeating. The rationalization inherent in organizations breeds constant attempts to bring areas of uncertainty within the range of formal controls, and experts are themselves agents of the rationalization that diminishes their own power. The more they succeed in recording their own know-how in bureaucratic procedures and regulations, the more their own power to deal with the uncertainties themselves is curtailed. Their choices become restricted. Therefore the maintenance workers in the tobacco factories strove to keep their rules of thumb to themselves and to prevent them becoming bureaucratized. Even though there were officially laid down instructions for the setting and maintenance of machines kept at head office in Paris, these were completely disregarded by the maintenance workers and there were no copies in the factories themselves. For *the routinization of uncertainty removes power.*

This shapes strategies up and down hierarchies as well as between occupational groupings. The battle between superiors and subordinates involves a basic strategy by which subordinates resist rules which encroach upon their discretion, whilst pressing for rules which will limit the discretion of their superiors over them.

It is possible for opposed strategies to interlock in a series of bureaucratic vicious circles which block change. Administrators try to extend bureaucratic regulation: those subjected to it resist. The directors of the tobacco factories typically pressed for the modernization of procedures, whilst the technical engineers resisted anything that might alter the position of their maintenance workers. Crozier sees French society as a whole as an example of this, for its tendencies to bureaucratic centralization and impersonality provoke protective strategies by those affected, and these strategies in turn provoke greater bureaucratization. In every branch of administration each level of hierarchy becomes a layer protected from those above and beneath. Those beneath restrict communication to those above and stall any threatening changes, while those above make ill-informed decisions which are not carried out as intended but from the consequences of which they are shielded.

This gives rise to a peculiar rhythm of change in bureaucratic organizations, certainly in France and perhaps elsewhere too. It is an alternation of long periods of stability with very short periods of crisis and change. Conflicts are stifled until they explode. Explosive crises are therefore endemic to such bureaucracies, and necessary to them as a means for change. At such times in French bureaucracies, personal authority supersedes the rules as someone, such as General de Gaulle, is able to force some change *out of the crisis. Authoritarian reformer figures* wait amid the bureaucratic routine for that moment of crisis when the system will need them.

Yet Crozier is optimistic. He hopes that if reforms were made in training and recruitment for French public administration, and in its caste system, the elites could be opened up. He argues that the large organizations of the modern world are not necessarily inimical to change, for change has never been faster and it is faster in those societies with the largest organizations. But there is always a risk that bureaucratic structures lead to forms of power game which block the changes that are needed.

BIBLIOGRAPHY

CROZIER, M., *The Bureaucratic Phenomenon*, Tavistock Publications and University of Chicago Press, 1964.

CROZIER, M., and FRIEDBERG, E., *Actors and Systems*, University of Chicago Press, 1980.

FIVE

People in Organizations

Management succeeds or fails in proportion as it is accepted without reservation by the group as authority and leader.
ELTON MAYO

The entire organization must consist of a multiple overlapping group structure with *every* work group using group decision-making processes skilfully.
RENSIS LIKERT

The average human being learns, under proper conditions, not only to accept but to seek responsibility.
DOUGLAS MCGREGOR

The successful manager must be a good diagnostician and must value a spirit of enquiry.
EDGAR H. SCHEIN

The primary functions of any organization, whether religious, political or industrial, should be to implement the needs of man to enjoy a meaningful existence.
FREDERICK HERZBERG

Only organizations based on the redundancy of functions (as opposed to the redundancy of parts) have the flexibility and innovative potential to give the possibility of adaptation to a rapid change rate, increasing complexity and environmental uncertainty.
ERIC TRIST

Organizations are systems of interdependent *human beings*. Although this has been recognized implicitly by the writers of the previous sections, and explicitly by some, their main concern has been with the 'formal system' – its aims, the principles on which it should be constituted to achieve them, and the methods by which it should function. People have then been considered as one of the essential resources required to achieve the aims. But people are a rather special sort of resource. They not only work for the organization – they *are* the organization.

The behaviour of the members of an organization clearly affects both its structure and its functioning, as well as the principles on which it can be managed. Most importantly, human beings affect the aims of organizations in which they participate – not merely the methods used to accomplish them. The writers in this chapter are social scientists who are specifically concerned to analyse the behaviour of people and its effects on all aspects of the organization. They have studied human attitudes, expectations, value systems, tensions and conflicts and the effects these have on productivity, adaptability, cohesion and morale. They have regarded the organization as a 'natural system' – an organism whose processes have to be studied in their own right – rather than as a 'formal system' – a mechanism designed to achieve particular ends.

Elton Mayo is the founding father of the 'Human Relations Movement' which brought into prominence the view that workers and managers must first be understood as human beings. Rensis Likert and Douglas McGregor reject the underlying assumptions about human behaviour on which formal organizations have been built and propose new methods of management based on a more adequate understanding of human motivation.

Edgar H. Schein's concern has been to understand and manage the relationship between the individual's career and the organization's culture, while Frederick Herzberg determines how people's characteristically human needs for growth and development may be satisfied in work.

Eric Trist and his colleagues at the Tavistock Institute demonstrate the utility of designing groups and organizations, which, while taking account of technical concerns, can also make provision for social and psychological aspects of human behaviour.

Elton Mayo and the Hawthorne Investigations

Elton Mayo (1880–1949) was an Australian who spent most of his working life at Harvard University, eventually becoming Professor of Industrial Research in the Graduate School of Business Administration. In this post he was responsible for the initiation and direction of many research projects, the most famous being the five-year investigation of the Hawthorne works of the Western Electric Company in Chicago. Immediately prior to his death, Mayo was consultant on industrial problems to the British Government.

Elton Mayo has often been called the founder of both the Human Relations Movement and of industrial sociology. The research that he directed showed the importance of groups in affecting the behaviour of individuals at work and enabled him to make certain deductions about what managers ought to do.

Like most of his contemporaries, Mayo's initial interests were in fatigue, accidents and labour turnover, and the effect on these of rest pauses and physical conditions of work. One of his first investigations was of a spinning mill in Philadelphia where labour turnover in one department was 250 per cent compared with an average of 6 per cent for all the other departments. Rest pauses were introduced by Mayo, and production and morale improved. When the operatives took part in fixing the frequency and duration of the pauses a further improvement was registered and morale in the whole factory also improved. At the end of the first year, turnover in the department concerned was down to the average for the rest of the mill. The initial explanation was that the rest pauses, in breaking up the monotony of the job, improved the mental and physical condition of the workers. However, after subsequent investigations, Mayo modified his explanation.

The major investigation which led to this modification and which laid

the basis for a great many subsequent studies was the Hawthorne Experiment, carried out between 1927 and 1932. Prior to the entry of Mayo's
team an inquiry had been made by a number of engineers into the effect
of illumination on workers and their work. Two groups of workers had
been isolated and the lighting conditions for one had been varied and for
the other held constant. No significant differences in output were found
between the two; indeed whatever was done with the lighting, production
rose in *both* groups.

At this point the Industrial Research team directed by Mayo took over.
The first stage of their inquiry is known as the Relay Assembly Test
Room. Six female operatives, engaged in assembling telephone relays,
were segregated in order to observe the effect on output and morale of
various changes in the conditions of work. During the five years of experiment various changes were introduced and a continuous record of
output was kept. At first a special group payment scheme was introduced:
previously the women had been grouped with one hundred other operatives for incentive payment purposes. Other changes introduced at various
times were rest pauses in several different forms (varying in length and
spacing), shorter hours and refreshments, in all more than ten changes.
Before putting the changes into effect, the investigators spent a lot of time
discussing them with the women. Communication between the workers
and the research team was very full and open throughout the experimental
period. Almost without exception output increased with each change
made.

The next stage in the experiment was to return to the original conditions. The operatives reverted to a forty-eight-hour six-day week, no incentive, no rest pauses and no refreshment. Output went up to the highest
yet recorded. By this time it had become clear, to quote Mayo, 'that the
itemized changes experimentally imposed . . . could not be used to explain the major change – the continually increasing production'. The
explanation eventually given was that the women experienced a tremendous increase in work satisfaction because they had greater freedom in
their working environment and control over their own pace-setting. The
six operatives had become a social group with their own standards and
expectations. By removing the women from the normal setting of work
and by intensifying their interaction and cooperation, informal practices,
values, norms and social relationships had been built up giving the group
high cohesion. Also, the communication system between the researchers

and the workers was extremely effective; this meant that the norms of output were those that the women felt the researchers desired. The supervisors took a personal interest in each worker and showed pride in the record of the group. The result was that the workers and the supervisors developed a sense of participation and as a result established a completely new working pattern. Mayo's generalization was that work satisfaction depends to a large extent on the informal social pattern of the work group. Where norms of cooperativeness and high output are established because of a feeling of importance, physical conditions have little impact.

However, this is the explanation arrived at in later years. At the time of the actual experiment, the continually increasing output was regarded as something of a mystery so an inquiry was instituted into conditions in the factory at large. This took the form of an interview programme. It was quickly realized that such a programme told the researchers little about the actual conditions in the factory but a great deal about the attitudes of various employees. The major finding of this stage of the inquiry was that many problems of worker–management cooperation were the results of the emotionally based attitudes of the workers rather than of objective difficulties in the situation. Workers, thought Mayo, were activated by a 'logic of sentiment', whereas management is concerned with the 'logic of cost and efficiency'. Conflict is inevitable unless this difference is understood and provided for.

The third stage of the investigation was to observe a group performing a task in a natural setting, i.e. a non-experimental situation. A number of male employees in what became known as the Bank Wiring Observation Room were put under constant observation and their output recorded. It was found that they restricted their output; the group had a standard for output and this was not exceeded by any individual worker. The attitude of the members of the group towards the company's financial incentive scheme was one of indifference. The group was highly integrated with its own social structure and code of behaviour which clashed with that of management. Essentially this code was composed of solidarity on the part of the group against management. Not too much work should be done, that would be ratebusting; on the other hand, not too little work should be done, that would be chiselling. There was little recognition of the organization's formal allocation of roles. This was confirmation of the importance of informal social groupings in determining levels of output.

Taken as a whole, the significance of the Hawthorne investigation was in 'discovering' the informal organization which, it is now realized, exists in all organizations. It demonstrated the importance to individuals of stable social relationships in the work situation. It confirmed Mayo in his wider thinking that what he calls the 'rabble hypothesis' about human behaviour (that each individual pursues only a narrow rational self-interest) was completely false. It confirmed his view that the breakdown of traditional values in society could be countered by creating a situation in industry conducive to spontaneous cooperation.

For Mayo, one of the major tasks of management is to organize spontaneous cooperation, thereby preventing the further breakdown of society. As traditional attachments to community and family disappear, and as the workplace increases in importance, the support given by traditional institutions must now be given by the organization. Conflict, competition and disagreement between individuals are to be avoided by management understanding its role as providing the basis for group affiliation. From the end of the Hawthorne project to his death Mayo was interested in discovering how spontaneous cooperation could be achieved. It is this which has been the basis of the Human Relations Movement – the use of the insights of the social sciences to secure the commitment of individuals to the ends and activities of the organization.

The impact of Hawthorne and Mayo on both management and academics has been tremendous. It led to a fuller realization and understanding of the 'human factor' in work situations. Central to this was the 'discovery' of the informal group as an outlet for the aspirations of the worker. His work also led to an emphasis on the importance of an adequate communication system, particularly upwards from workers to management. The investigation showed, to quote Mayo, that 'management succeeds or fails in proportion as it is accepted without reservation by the group as authority and leader.'

BIBLIOGRAPHY

MAYO, E., *The Human Problems of an Industrial Civilization*, Macmillan, 1933.
MAYO, E., *The Social Problems of an Industrial Civilization*, Routledge & Kegan Paul, 1949.
ROETHLISBERGER, F. J., and DICKSON, W. J., *Management and the Worker*, Harvard University Press, 1949.

Rensis Likert and Douglas McGregor

Rensis Likert (1903–81) was an American social psychologist who in 1949 established the Institute of Social Research at the University of Michigan. Until his retirement in 1969, he was thus at the head of one of the major institutions conducting research into human behaviour in organizations. On his retirement he formed Rensis Likert Associates, a consulting firm, to put his ideas about the management of organizations into wider practice. His books are based on the numerous research studies which he and his colleagues have conducted. His last book was jointly written with his research collaborator and wife, Jane Gibson Likert.

Douglas McGregor (1906–64) was a social psychologist who published a number of research papers in this field. For some years he was President (i.e. Chief Executive) of Antioch College and he has described how this period as a top administrator affected his views on organizational functioning. From 1954 until his death, he was Professor of Management at the Massachusetts Institute of Technology.

'Managers with the best records of performance in American business and government are in the process of pointing the way to an appreciably more effective system of management than now exists,' proclaims Likert. Research studies have shown that departments which are low in efficiency tend to be in the charge of supervisors who are 'job-centred'. That is, they 'tend to concentrate on keeping their subordinates busily engaged in going through a specified work cycle in a prescribed way and at a satisfactory rate as determined by time standards'. This attitude is clearly derived from that of Taylor (see p. 102), with its emphasis on breaking down the job into component parts, selecting and training people to do them, and exerting constant pressure to achieve output. Supervisors see themselves as getting the job done with the resources (which include the people) at their disposal.

Supervisors with the best record of performance are found to focus their attention on the human aspects of their subordinates' problems, and on building effective work groups which are set high achievement goals. These supervisors are 'employee-centred'. They regard their jobs as dealing with human beings rather than with the work; they attempt to know them as individuals. They see their function as helping them to do the job efficiently. They exercise general rather than detailed supervision, and are more concerned with targets than methods. They allow maximum participation in decision-making. If high performance is to be obtained, a supervisor must not only be employee-centred but must also have high performance goals and be capable of exercising the decision-making processes to achieve them.

In summarizing these findings, Likert distinguishes four systems of management. System 1 is the exploitive authoritative type where management uses fear and threats, communication is downward, superiors and subordinates are psychologically far apart, and the bulk of decisions are taken at the top of the organization. System 2 is the benevolent authoritative type where management uses rewards, subordinates' attitudes are subservient to superiors, information flowing upward is restricted to what the boss wants to hear, policy decisions are taken at the top but decisions within a prescribed framework may be delegated to lower levels. System 3 is the consultative type where management uses rewards, occasional punishments, and some involvement is sought; communication is both down and up but upward communication other than that which the boss wants to hear is given in limited amounts and only cautiously. In this system subordinates can have a moderate amount of influence on the activities of their departments as broad policy decisions are taken at the top and more specific decisions at lower levels.

System 4 is characterized by participative group management. Management gives economic rewards and makes full use of group participation and involvement in setting high performance goals, and improving work methods; communication flows downwards, upwards and with peers, and is accurate; subordinates and superiors are very close psychologically. Decision-making is widely done throughout the organization through group processes, and is integrated into the formal structure by regarding the organization chart as a series of overlapping groups with each group linked to the rest of the organization by means of persons (called 'linking pins') who are members of more than one group. System 4 management produces high productivity, greater involvement of individuals, and better labour–management relations.

In general, high-producing managers are those who have built the personnel in their units into effective groups, whose members have cooperative attitudes and a high level of job satisfaction through System 4 management. But there are exceptions. Technically competent, job-centred, tough management can achieve high productivity (particularly if backed up by tight systems of control techniques). But the members of units whose supervisors use these high-pressure methods are likely to have unfavourable attitudes towards their work and the management, and to have excessively high levels of waste and scrap. They also show higher labour turnover, and greater labour–management conflict as measured by work-stoppages, official grievances and the like.

Management, according to Likert, is always a relative process. To be effective and to communicate, leaders must always adapt their behaviour to take account of the persons whom they lead. There are no specific rules which will work well in all situations, but only general principles which must be interpreted to take account of the expectations, values and skills of those with whom the manager interacts. Sensitivity to these values and expectations is a crucial leadership skill, and organizations must create the atmosphere and conditions which encourage all managers to deal with the people they encounter in a manner fitting to their values and their expectations.

To assist in this task, management now has available a number of measures of relevant factors which have been developed by social scientists. Methods are available to obtain objective measurements of such variables as: the amount of member loyalty to an organization; the extent to which the goals of groups and individuals facilitate the achievement of the organization's goals; the level of motivation among members; the degree of confidence and trust between different hierarchical levels and between different sub-units; the efficiency and adequacy of the communication process; the extent to which superiors are correctly informed of the expectations, reactions, obstacles, problems and failures of subordinates – together with the assistance they find useful and the assurance they wish they could get.

These measures and others enable an organization to know at any time the state of the system of functioning human beings which underpins it (called the 'interaction-influence system'); whether it is improving or deteriorating and why, and what to do to bring about desired improvements. This objective information about the interaction-influence system enables problems of leadership and management to be depersonalized and the 'authority of facts' to come to the fore. A much wider range of human behaviour can now be measured and made objective, whereas previously impressions and judgements had to suffice.

Douglas McGregor examines the assumptions about human behaviour which underlie managerial action. The traditional conception of administration (as exemplified by the writings of Fayol, p. 97) is based upon the direction and control by management of the enterprise and its individual members. It implies certain basic assumptions about human motivation, which McGregor characterizes as 'Theory X'. These are:

1. The average human being has an inherent dislike of work and will avoid it if possible. Thus management needs to stress productivity, incentive schemes and a 'fair day's work'; and to denounce 'restriction of output'.
2. Because of this human characteristic of dislike of work, most people must be coerced, controlled, directed, threatened with punishment to get them to put forth adequate effort toward the achievement of organizational objectives.
3. The average human being prefers to be directed, wishes to avoid responsibility, has relatively little ambition, wants security above all.

Theory X has persisted for a long time (although it is not usually stated as baldly as this). It has done so because it has undoubtedly provided an explanation for *some* human behaviour in organizations. There are, however, many readily observable facts and a growing body of research findings (such as those described by Likert) which cannot be explained on these assumptions. McGregor proposes an alternative 'Theory Y', with the underlying principle of 'integration' to replace direction and control. The assumptions about human motivation of Theory Y are:

1. The expenditure of physical and mental effort in work is as natural as play or rest. The ordinary person does not inherently dislike work: according to the conditions it may be a source of satisfaction or punishment.
2. External control is not the only means for obtaining effort. People will exercise self-direction and self-control in the service of objectives to which they are committed.

3. The most significant reward that can be offered in order to obtain commitment is the satisfaction of the individual's 'self-actualizing needs' (see Schein, p. 168). This can be a direct product of effort directed towards organizational objectives.
4. The average human being learns, under proper conditions, not only to accept but to seek responsibility.
5. Many more people are able to contribute creatively to the solution of organizational problems than do so.
6. At present the potentialities of the average person are not being fully used.

McGregor develops an analysis of how the acceptance of Theory Y as the basis for running organizations would work out. He is particularly concerned with effects on performance appraisals, salaries and promotions, participation and staff–line relationships. On this last topic he makes the important point that there will be tension and conflict between staff and line as long as the staff departments are used as a service to top management to *control* the line (which is required by Theory X). With Theory Y the role of the staff is regarded as that of providing professional help to *all levels* of management.

The essential concept which both Likert and McGregor are propounding is that modern organizations, to be effective, must regard themselves as interacting groups of people with '*supportive relationships*' to each other. In the ideal, all members will feel that the organization's objectives are of personal significance to them. They will regard their jobs, which contribute to the objectives, as meaningful, indispensable and difficult. Therefore, in order to do their jobs effectively, they need and obtain the support of their superiors. Superiors in turn regard their prime function as the giving of this support to make their subordinates effective.

In later work Likert and Likert extend the System 1 to 4 classification by identifying the 'System 4 Total Model Organization' (System 4T). This designation refers to organizations which have a number of characteristics in addition to those of System 4. These include: high levels of performance goals held by the leader and transmitted to subordinates; high levels of knowledge and skill of the leader with regard to technical issues, administration and problem-solving; the capacity of the leader to provide planning, resources, equipment, training and help to subordinates. System 4T is also characterized by optimum structure in terms of differentiation and linkages, and stable group working relationships.

System 4T is currently the best method for dealing with conflict because of its approach of getting appropriate data related to *group* needs (thus removing person-to-person conflict) and engaging in group decision-making in order to resolve the differences in the best interests of the entire organization. If members of one or both of the two groups show an inability to use group decision-making techniques sufficiently well, then higher levels must provide further training in group processes. The interaction-influence system will develop a capacity for self-correction, since superiors recognize those groups which are not performing their linking-pin and problem-solving functions effectively and can arrange for coaching and training. Correction is possible because the failures are picked up not by after-the-fact data (e.g. falling production, rising costs, lower earnings) but through the interaction-influence system, in the early stages before poor performance and conflict arise.

Likert's argument is that the nearer to System 4T the organization approaches the more productivity and profits will improve and conflict be reduced. Likert also suggests a System 5 organization of the future in which the authority of hierarchy will completely disappear. The authority of individuals will derive only from their linking-pin roles and from the influence exerted by the overlapping groups of which they are members.

BIBLIOGRAPHY

LIKERT, R., *New Patterns of Management*, McGraw-Hill, 1961.

LIKERT, R., *The Human Organization: Its Management and Value*, McGraw-Hill, 1967.

MCGREGOR, D., *The Human Side of Enterprise*, McGraw-Hill, 1960.

MCGREGOR, D., *Leadership and Motivation*, MIT Press, 1966.

MCGREGOR, D., *The Professional Manager*, McGraw-Hill, 1967.

LIKERT, R., and LIKERT, J. G., *New Ways of Managing Conflict*, McGraw-Hill, 1976.

Edgar H. Schein

Edgar H. Schein has been for many years Professor of Management at the Sloan School of Management of the Massachusetts Institute of Technology. A social psychologist by training, in his early years at MIT he was a junior colleague of Douglas McGregor (see p. 161) whose personality and work had much influence on him. Working in that tradition, Schein has been an influential researcher, consultant and writer on issues concerned with organizational behaviour, particularly individual motivation, career dynamics and organizational culture.

Schein's analysis of motivation begins, like McGregor's, with an examination of the underlying assumptions that managers make about the people they manage. He suggests three sets of assumptions, roughly in order of their historical appearance, and adds a fourth which he considers more appropriate.

1. The *Rational-Economic Model* is the mental picture held by managers who consider workers to be primarily motivated by economic incentives as manipulated by the organization. The worker is essentially passive, lazy, unwilling to take responsibility and must therefore be controlled by the manager. This is the basis of Taylor's approach to management (see p. 102), which is expounded by McGregor (see p. 164) as Theory X. This approach led to the possibility of mass-production industry, but broke down when unions became powerful, and jobs became more complex requiring more of an employee than being just a 'pair of hands'.

2. The *Social Model* developed from awareness of the worker's needs for identity through relationships with others, particularly the working group. The group's norms and pressures have much more power over production than do formal incentive systems and management controls. The work of Mayo and the Hawthorne investigations (see p. 157) had an important impact in changing managerial ideas, as did the study

by Trist and his colleagues of mining (see p. 177). The implications for managers are spelled out in Likert's work on the need for 'employee-centred' leadership and participative group management (see p. 161).

3. The *Self-Actualizing Model* is a further development which underlines that typically organizations remove the meaning of any work that employees do. The inherent need of workers to exercise their understanding, capacities and skills in an adult way is thus frustrated, and alienation and dissatisfaction ensue. The analysis of the clinical psychologist, Abraham Maslow, has been very influential here. He maintains that 'self-actualization' (the realization of one's distinctive psychological potential) is the highest form of human need, going beyond economic and social fulfilment. The implications of this approach are developed for managers in McGregor's Theory Y (see p. 164), Argyris's Model II (see p. 201) and Herzberg's Job Enrichment (see p. 174).

4. The *Complex Model*, developed by Schein, maintains that earlier theories are based on conceptions which are too simplified and generalized. Human needs fall into many categories and vary according to the person's stage of personal development and life situation. So motives will vary from one person to another, one situation to another, one time to another. Incentives can also vary in their impact: money, for example, usually satisfying basic economic needs can also serve to satisfy self-actualization needs for some. What motivates millionaires to go on to make their second or fifth million? Employees are also capable of learning new motives through organizational experiences, and can respond to different kinds of managerial strategies.

The most important implication for managers is that they need to be good diagnosticians. They should be flexible enough to vary their own behaviour in relation to the need to treat in an appropriate way particular subordinates in particular situations. They may use any of the economic, social or self-actualizing models. They may use 'scientific management' in the design of some jobs, but allow complete group autonomy for the workers to organize themselves in others. They would thus use a 'contingency approach', as exemplified by Lawrence and Lorsch (see p. 58) and Vroom (see p. 143).

According to Schein, the key factor which determines the motivation of individuals in organizations is the psychological contract. This is the unwritten set of expectations operating at all times between every member of an organization and those who represent the organization itself to that member. It includes economic components (pay, working hours, job security, etc.) but it will also include more implicit concerns such as being treated with dignity, obtaining some degree of work autonomy, having opportunities to learn and develop. Some of the strongest feelings leading to strikes and employee turnover have to do with violations of these implicit components, even though the public negotiations are about pay and conditions of work.

The organization, too, has implicit expectations: that employees will be loyal, will keep trade secrets, and will do their best on behalf of the organization. Whether individuals will work with commitment and enthusiasm is the result of a matching between the two components. On the one side, their own expectations of what the organization will provide for them and what they should provide in return; on the other, the organization's expectations of what it will give and get. The degree to which these correspond will determine the individual's motivation. The degree of matching is liable to change and the psychological contract is therefore continually being renegotiated, particularly during the progress of an individual's career.

The 'career development perspective' taken by Schein sees the continual matching process between the individual and the organization as the key to understanding both human resource planning for the organization and career planning for the individual. This matching is particularly important at certain key transitions in a career, such as initial entry into the organization, moving from technical to managerial work, changing from being 'on the way up' to 'levelling off' and so on.

A crucial element in the matching is the nature of the *career anchor* that the individual holds. This is the self-perceived set of talents, motives and attitudes, based on actual experience, which is developed by each individual particularly in the early years of an organizational career. It provides a growing area of stability within the individual's attitudes which anchors the interpretation of career and life options. Typical career anchors found by Schein in a detailed longitudinal study of MIT management graduates include those of technical competence, managerial competence, security and autonomy. Career anchors affect considerably the way individuals see themselves, their jobs and their organizations. For example, one graduate using a technical competence anchor was still, in mid-career, only concerned with technical tasks. He refused to become involved in aspects of sales or general management even though he was now a director and part owner of the firm in which he worked. Another graduate, using managerial competence as an anchor, left one firm although his bosses were quite pleased with his performance. But he considered that he only actually worked two hours a day, and he was not satisfied with that.

The understanding of the dynamics of career development is important in enabling Human Resource Planning and Development to improve the matching processes between individual and organization needs so that early-, mid- and late-career crises can be dealt with more effectively.

A distinctive aspect of the way that an organization functions, which shapes its overall performance as well as the feelings which individuals have about it, is its culture. This is the pattern of basic assumptions developed by an organization as it learns to cope with problems of external adaptation and internal integration. These assumptions are taught to new members as the correct way to perceive, think and feel in order to be successful. They cover a wide range of issues: how to dress, how much to argue, how far to defer to the boss's authority, what to reward and what to punish, are some of them. Organizations develop very wide differences on these topics.

Leaders play a key role in maintaining and transmitting the culture. They do this by a number of powerful mechanisms. What they pay attention to, measure and control; how they react to a range of crises; who they recruit, promote, excommunicate; all these send important messages about the kind of organization they are running. The key to leadership is managing cultural change.

The considerable difficulties that almost inevitably beset the establishment of an effective organization after a merger of two companies underline the need to understand the nature of cultural differences and how cultural change can be consciously managed. The big danger is that the acquiring company will not only impose its own structures and procedures but also its own philosophy, value systems and managerial style on a situation for which it has no intuitive 'feel'. Thus, a large packaged-foods manufacturer purchased a chain of successful fast-food restaurants. They imposed many of their manufacturing control procedures on the new subsidiary, which drove costs up and restaurant managers out. These were replaced by parent-company managers who did not really understand the technology and hence were unable to make effective use of the marketing techniques. Despite ten years of effort they could not run it profitably and had to sell it at a considerable loss.

Similar problems occur when organizations diversify into new product lines, new areas or new markets. Afterwards managers frequently say that cultural incompatibilities were at the root of the troubles, but somehow these factors rarely get taken into account at the time. One reason is that the culture of an organization is so pervasive that it is very difficult for members to identify its components in their own situation. They only recognize their own characteristics when they run up against problems due to differences in others. Schein presents a series of diagnostic procedures which would enable managers (usually with the help of an outside consultant) to uncover the cultural assumptions of their own organization and thus gain insight into its compatibility with others.

BIBLIOGRAPHY

SCHEIN, E. H., *Organizational Psychology*, 3rd edn, Prentice-Hall, 1980.

SCHEIN, E. H., *Career Dynamics: Matching Individual and Organizational Needs*, Addison-Wesley, 1978.

SCHEIN, E. H., *Organizational Culture and Leadership*, Jossey-Bass, 1985.

Frederick Herzberg

Frederick Herzberg is Distinguished Professor of Management in the University of Utah. After training as a psychologist he studied Industrial Mental Health. For many years he has, with colleagues and students, been conducting a programme of research and application on human motivation in the work situation and its effects on the individual's job satisfaction and mental health. He questions whether current methods of organizing work in business and industry are appropriate for people's total needs and happiness.

Herzberg and his colleagues conducted a survey of 200 engineers and accountants representing a cross-section of Pittsburgh industry. They were asked to remember times when they felt exceptionally good about their jobs. The investigators probed for the reasons why they felt as they did, asking for a description of the sequence of events which gave that feeling. The questions were then repeated for sequences of events which made them feel exceptionally bad about their jobs. The responses were then classified by topic in order to determine what type of events led to job satisfaction and job dissatisfaction.

The major finding of the study was that the events that led to satisfaction were of quite a different kind from those that led to dissatisfaction. Five factors stood out as strong determinants of job satisfaction: achievement, recognition, the attraction of the work itself, responsibility, and advancement. Lack of these five factors, though, was mentioned very infrequently in regard to job *dis*satisfaction. When the reasons for the dissatisfaction were analysed they were found to be concerned with a different range of factors: company policy and administration, supervision, salary, interpersonal relations and working conditions. Since such distinctly separate factors were found to be associated with job satisfaction and job dissatisfaction, Herzberg concludes that these two feelings are not the opposites to one another, rather they are concerned with two different ranges of human needs.

The set of factors associated with job dissatisfaction are those stemming from the individual's overriding need to avoid physical and social deprivation. Using a biblical analogy, Herzberg relates these to the 'Adam' conception of the nature of humanity. When Adam was expelled from the Garden of Eden he was immediately faced with the task of satisfying the needs which stem from his animal nature: the needs for food, warmth, avoidance of pain, safety, security, belongingness, etc. Ever since then people have had to concern themselves with the satisfaction of these needs together with those which, as a result of social conditioning, have been added to them. Thus, for example, we have learned that in certain economies the satisfaction of these needs makes it necessary to earn money which has therefore become a specific motivating drive.

In contrast, the factors associated with job satisfaction are those stemming from people's need to realize their human potential for perfection In biblical terms this is the 'Abraham' conception of human nature. Abraham was created in the image of God. He was capable of great accomplishments, of development, of growth, of transcending his environmental limitations, of self-realization. People have these aspects to their natures too; they are indeed the characteristically human ones. They have needs to understand, to achieve, and through achievement to experience psychological growth, and these needs are very powerful motivating drives.

Both the Adam and Abraham natures look for satisfaction in work, but they do so in different ranges of factors. The Adam nature seeks the avoidance of dissatisfaction and is basically concerned with the job environment. It requires effective company policies, working conditions, security, pay, etc. and is affected by inadequacies in these. Since they are extrinsic to the job itself, Herzberg refers to them as 'job hygiene' or 'maintenance' factors. Just as lack of hygiene will cause disease but the presence of hygienic conditions will not, of itself, produce health, so lack of adequate 'job hygiene' factors will cause dissatisfaction, but their presence will not of itself cause satisfaction. Satisfaction in work is provided through the Abraham nature which is concerned with the job content of the work itself, with achievement, recognition, responsibility, advancement, etc. These are the motivator or growth factors and their presence will cause satisfaction. Their absence will not cause dissatisfaction (if the job hygiene factors are adequate) but will lead to an absence of positive satisfactions. It is thus basic to Herzberg's approach that job satisfaction and job dissatisfaction are not opposites, since they are concerned with different factors in work serving different aspects of human nature. The opposite of job satisfaction, therefore, is not job dissatisfaction but simply no job satisfaction. The opposite of job dissatisfaction, similarly, is lack of job dissatisfaction.

This finding of the original study – that the factors associated with job satisfaction were basically different in kind from those associated with job dissatisfaction – has been repeated in several subsequent studies. Collating the information based on twelve different investigations, involving over 1,600 employees in a variety of jobs in business and other organizations and in a number of countries, Herzberg presents results to show that the overwhelming majority of the factors contributing to job satisfaction (81 per cent) were the motivators concerned with growth and development. A large majority of the factors contributing to job dissatisfaction (69 per cent) involved hygiene or environmental maintenance.

How, then, may this 'motivation-hygiene' approach be used to increase the motivation and job satisfaction of employees? First, it is clear that this cannot be done through the job hygiene factors. Certainly, these can and should be improved as they will reduce job dissatisfaction, but adequate company policies, working conditions, pay and supervision, are increasingly thought of as a right to be expected, not as an incentive to greater achievement and satisfaction. For this, the rewarding nature of the work itself, recognition, responsibility, opportunities for achievement and advancement are necessary. Herzberg recognizes that these are phrases that may be used nowadays in relation to jobs, but they are often used in a superficial way, or as inspirational talk without much effective action. He therefore advocates an industrial engineering approach, based on the design of jobs, but from the opposite point of view from that of Taylor (see p. 102). Instead of rationalizing and simplifying the work to increase efficiency, the motivation-hygiene theory suggests that jobs be enriched to include the motivating factors in order to bring about an effective utilization of people and to increase job satisfaction.

The principles of *job enrichment* require that the job be developed to include new aspects which provide the opportunity for the employee's psychological growth. It is important that the new aspects are capable of allowing this. Merely to add one undemanding job to another (as is often the case with job enlargement) or to switch from one undemanding job to another (as in job rotation) is not adequate. These are merely horizontal job loading. In contrast, job enrichment calls for vertical job loading, where opportunities for achievement, responsibility, recognition, growth and learning are designed into the job. The approach would be to look for ways of removing some controls while retaining or increasing individuals' accountability for their own work; giving a person a complete natural unit of work; granting additional authority to an employee in the job; increasing job freedom; making reports directly available to the worker personally rather than to the supervisor; introducing new and more difficult tasks not previously undertaken, etc.

A number of experiments have been reported by Herzberg and his colleagues where these changes have been introduced with considerable effect. For example, in a study of the job of 'stockholder correspondent' of a large corporation the following suggestions were considered but rejected as involving merely horizontal job loading. In m fixed quotas could be set for letters to be answered each day, the employees could type the letters themselves as well as composing them, all difficult inquiries could be channelled to a few workers so that the rest could achieve high rates of output, the workers could be rotated through units handling different inquiries and then sent back to their own units. Instead, changes leading to the enrichment of jobs were introduced, such as: correspondents were made directly responsible for the quality and accuracy of letters which were sent out directly over their names (previously a verifier had checked all letters, the supervisor had rechecked and signed them and was responsible for their quality and accuracy), subject-matter experts were appointed within each unit for other members to consult (previously the supervisor had dealt with all difficult and specialized questions), verification of experienced workers' letters was dropped from 100 per cent to 10 per cent and correspondents were encouraged to answer letters in a more personalized way instead of relying upon standard forms. In these ways, the jobs were enriched with resulting increases in both performance and job satisfaction.

In other studies, laboratory technicians ('experimental officers') were encouraged to write personal project reports in addition to those of the supervising scientists and were authorized to requisition materials and equipment direct; sales representatives were made wholly responsible for determining the calling frequencies on their customers and were given a discretionary range of about 10 per cent on the prices of most products; factory supervisors were authorized to modify schedules, to hire labour against agreed manning targets, to appoint their deputies, and so on. In each case, the results in both performance and satisfaction were considerable.

The more subordinates' jobs become enriched, the more superfluous does 'on the job' supervision in the old sense become. But this does not downgrade the supervisors' job; in the companies studied they found themselves free to develop more important aspects of their jobs with a greater managerial component than they had had time to before. It soon becomes clear that supervising people who have authority of their own is a more demanding, rewarding and enjoyable task than checking on every move of circumscribed automatons. For management the challenge is task organization to call out the motivators, and task support to provide adequate hygiene through company policy, technical supervision, working conditions, etc., thus satisfying both the Adam and the Abraham natures of humanity in work.

BIBLIOGRAPHY

HERZBERG, F., *Work and the Nature of Man*, World Publishing Co., 1966.

HERZBERG, F., 'One more time: How do you motivate employees?' *Harvard Business Review* 46 (1968), 53–62.

HERZBERG, F., *Managerial Choice: To Be Efficient and To Be Human*, Dow Jones-Irwin, 1976.

HERZBERG, F., MAUSNER, B., and SNYDERMAN, B., *The Motivation to Work*, Wiley, 1959.

PAUL, W. J., JR, ROBERTSON, K. B., and HERZBERG, F., 'Job enrichment pays off', *Harvard Business Review* 47 (1969), 61–78.

Eric Trist and the Work of the Tavistock Institute

Eric Trist (1909–93) was a social psychologist who for over twenty years was the senior member of the Tavistock Institute of Human Relations, London, a leading centre for the application of social science to social and industrial problems. He was subsequently a professor at the University of Pennsylvania, and at York University, Ontario. At the Tavistock he conducted, with a number of colleagues (including F. E. Emery, A. K. Rice and E. J. Miller), a programme of combined research and consultancy investigations into group and organizational functioning. This combination of research and consultancy is referred to as 'action research' The work of Trist and his colleagues uses a systems approach to understanding organizational behaviour.

In collaboration with K. W. Bamforth (an ex-miner) Trist studied the effects of mechanization in British coal mining. With the advent of coal-cutters and mechanical conveyors, the degree of technical complexity of coal-getting was raised to a higher level. Mechanization made possible the working of a single long face in place of a series of short faces, but this technological change had a number of social and psychological consequences for the work organization and the worker's place in it, to which little thought was given before the change was introduced. The pattern of organization in short-face working was based on a small artisan group of a skilled man and his mate, assisted by one or more labourers. The basic pattern around which the work relationships in the longwall method were organized is the coal-face group of forty to fifty men, their shot-firer and 'deputies' (i.e. supervisors). Thus the basic unit in mining took on the characteristics in size and structure of a small factory department, and in doing so disrupted the traditional high degree of job autonomy and close work relationships with a number of deleterious effects.

The mass-production character of the longwall method necessitates a large-scale mobile layout advancing along the seam, basic task specialization according to shift, and very specific job roles with different methods of payment within each shift. In these circumstances there are considerable problems of maintaining effective communications and good working relations between forty men spatially spread over 200 yards in a tunnel, and temporally spread over twenty-four hours in three successive shifts. From the production engineering point of view it is possible to write an equation that 200 tons equals 40 men over 200 yards over 24 hours, but the psychological and social problems raised are of a new order when the work organization transcends the limits of the traditional small face-to-face group undertaking the complete task itself. The social integration of the previous small groups having been disrupted by the new technology, and little attempt made to achieve any new integration, many symptoms of social stress occur. Informal cliques which develop to help each other out can only occur over small parts of the face, inevitably leaving some isolated; individuals react defensively using petty deceptions with regard to time-keeping and reporting of work; they compete for allocation to the best workplaces; there is mutual scapegoating across shifts, each blaming the other for inadequacies (since in the new system with its decreased autonomy, no one individual can normally be pinpointed with the blame, scapegoating of the absent shift becomes self-perpetuating and resolves nothing). Absenteeism becomes a way of the miner compensating himself for the difficulties of the job.

This study of the effects of technological change led Trist to develop the concept of the working group as being neither a technical system nor a social system, but as an interdependent socio-technical system. The technological demands place limits on the type of work organization possible, but the work organization has social and psychological properties of its own that are independent of the technology. From this point of view it makes as little sense to regard social relationships as being determined by the technology as it does to regard the manner in which a job is performed as being determined by the social-psychological characteristics of the workers. The social and technical requirements are mutually interactive and they must also have economic validity, which is a third interdependent aspect. The attainment of optimum conditions for any one of these aspects does not necessarily result in optimum conditions for the system as a whole, since interference will occur if the others are inadequate. The aim should be joint optimization.

In further studies of mining, Trist found that it was possible, within the same technological and economic constraints, to operate different systems of work organization with different social and psychological effects, thus underlining the considerable degree of organizational choice which is available to management to enable them to take account of the social and psychological aspects. A third form of operation known as the 'composite longwall method' was developed, which enabled mining to benefit from the new technology while at the same time allowing some of the characteristics of the shortwall method to be continued. In the composite system, groups of men are responsible for the whole task, allocate themselves to shifts and to jobs within the shift, and are paid on a group bonus. Thus the problems of over-specialized work roles, segregation of tasks across shifts with consequent scapegoating and lack of group cohesion were overcome. For example, it became common for a sub-group that had finished its scheduled work for a shift before time, to carry on with the next activity in the sequence in order to help those men on the subsequent shift who were members of their group. The composite longwall method was quite comparable in technological terms with the conventional longwall method, but it led to greater productivity, lower cost, considerably less absenteeism and accidents and greater work satisfaction, since it was a socio-technical system which was better geared to the workers' social and psychological needs for job autonomy and close working relationships.

This socio-technical system approach was also applied to supervisory roles by Rice in studies of an Indian textile firm. He found that it was not enough to allocate to the supervisor a list of responsibilities (see Fayol, p. 97) and perhaps insist upon a particular style of handling workers (see Likert, p. 161). The supervisor's problems arise from a need to control and coordinate a system of worker–task relationships, and in particular to manage the 'boundary conditions', that is, those activities of this system which relate it to the larger system of which it is a part. In order to do this effectively, it is necessary to have an easily identifiable arrangement of tasks so that it is possible to maximize the autonomous responsibility of the group itself for its own internal control, thus freeing the supervisor for the key task of boundary management.

In an automatic weaving shed for example, in which the occupational roles had remained unchanged since hand weaving, the activities of the shed were broken down into component tasks, with the number of workers required determined by work studies of the separate tasks. Those in different occupational tasks worked on different numbers of looms; weavers operated twenty-four or thirty-two, battery fillers charged the batteries of forty-eight, smash hands served seventy-five, jobbers 112, the bobbin carrier 224, etc. This resulted in the shift manager having to inter-act about the job regularly with all the remaining twenty-eight workers on the shift, jobbers having to interact with fourteen, smash hands with nine, a weaver with seven, etc., all on the basis of individual interactions aggregated together only at the level of the whole shift, with no stable internal group structure. Rice carried through a reorganization to create four groups of six workers, each with a group leader, each with an identi-fiable group task and a new set of interdependent work roles to carry it out. The boundaries of these groups were more easily delineated, and thus the work leader's task in their management facilitated. As a result there was a considerable and sustained improvement in efficiency and decrease in damage.

These studies and others of the Tavistock Institute have led Emery and Trist to conceptualize the enterprise as an 'open socio-technical system'. 'Open' because it is a system concerned with obtaining inputs from its environment and exporting outputs to its environment, as well as operat-ing the conversion process in between. They regard the organization not in terms of a closed physical system which can obtain a stable resolution of forces in static equilibrium, but in the light of the biological concept of an open system (due to von Bertalanffy) in which the equilibrium obtained by the organism or the organization is essentially dynamic, having a continual interchange across the boundaries with its environ-ment. Indeed, they would regard the primary task of the management of the enterprise as a whole as that of relating the total system to its en-vironment through the regulation of the boundary interchanges, rather than that of internal regulation. A management which takes its environ-ment as given and concentrates on organizing internally in the most efficient way is pursuing a dangerous course. This does not mean that top management should not be involved in internal problems, but that such involvement must be oriented to the environmental opportunities and demands.

The problem is that environments are changing at an increasing rate and towards increasing complexity. Factors in the environment, over which the organization has no control or even no knowledge, may interact to cause significant changes. Emery and Trist have classified environments according to their degree of complexity from that of a placid, randomized environment (corresponding to the economist's perfect competition) to that of a 'turbulent field' in which significant variances arise not only from competitive organizations involved but also from the field (e.g. market) itself.

They present a case history of an organization which failed to appreciate that its environment was changing from a relatively placid to a relatively turbulent one. This company in the British food-canning industry had, for a long period, held 65 per cent of the market for its main product – a tinned vegetable. On this basis the company invested in a new automatic factory, and in doing so incorporated an inbuilt rigidity – the necessity for long runs. But even while the factory was being built, several changes in the environment were taking place over which the organization had no control. The development of frozen foods, and the increasing affluence which enabled more people to afford these, presented consumers with an alternative. Greater direct competition came from the existence of surplus crops which American frozen-food manufacturers sold off very cheaply due to their inappropriateness for freezing, their use by a number of small British *fruit*-canning firms with surplus capacity due to the seasonal nature of imported fruit, and the development of supermarkets and chain stores with a wish to sell more goods under their house names. As the small canners provided an extremely cheap article (having no marketing costs and a cheaper raw material) they were able within three years to capture over 50 per cent of a shrinking market through supermarket own-label channels. This is a clear example of the way in which factors in the environment interact directly to produce a considerable turbulence in the field of the organization's operations, which, in the case of the vegetable canning factory, required a large redefinition of the firm's purpose, market and product mix before a new dynamic equilibrium was obtained.

Emery and Trist maintain that enterprises like the food canner are designing their organization structures to be appropriate to simpler environments rather than the complex turbulent ones which they are actually facing. A new *design principle* is now required. Organizations by their very nature require what is known in systems theory and information theory as 'redundancy'. By this is meant duplication, replaceability, interchangeability, and these resources are needed to reduce error in the face of variability and change. The traditional technocratic bureaucracy is based on *redundancy of parts*. The parts are broken down so that the ultimate elements are as simple as possible; thus an unskilled worker in a narrow job who is cheap to replace and who takes little time to train would be regarded as an ideal job design. But this approach also requires reliable control systems – often cumbersome and costly.

An alternative design, based on the *redundancy of functions*, is appropriate to turbulent environments. In this approach individuals and units have wide repertoires of activities to cope with change and they are self-regulating. For the individual they create roles rather than mere jobs; for the organization, they bring into being a *variety-increasing* system rather than the traditional control by variety reduction. For this approach to be achieved there has to be continuing development of appropriate new values concerned with improving the *quality of working life* by keeping the technological determinants of worker behaviour to a minimum in order to satisfy social and psychological needs by the involvement of all. Autonomous working groups, collaboration rather than competition (between organizations as well as within them) and reduction of hierarchical emphasis, are some of the requirements for operating effectively in modern turbulence. The table opposite sets out the key features of the old and new approaches.

The socio-technical systems approach to jointly achieving effective functioning in a turbulent environment, and to increasing the quality of working life, has also been undertaken at a wider 'macro-social' level. For example, working with the Norwegian social psychologists E. Thorsrud and P. G. Herbst, the Tavistock group have studied the Norwegian shipping industry.

Many technological designs are available for sophisticated bulk carriers. The one chosen was that which best met the social and psychological needs of the small shipboard community that had to live together in isolated conditions, twenty-four hours a day for considerable periods, while efficiently achieving the work tasks. A common mess and a recreation room were established; deck and engine-room crews were integrated, status differences between officers and men were reduced and even eliminated through the development of open career lines and the establishment of 'all officer' ships. Also, training for future jobs onshore could be begun at sea.

Without these improvements in the quality of working life, not enough Norwegians would have gone to sea to sustain the Norwegian Merchant

Features of Old and New Approaches

Old Approach	New Approach
The technological imperative	Joint optimization
People as extensions of machines	People as complementary to machines
People as expendable spare parts	People as a resource to be developed
Maximum task breakdown, simple narrow skills	Optimum task grouping, multiple broad skills
External controls (supervisors, specialist staffs, procedures)	Internal controls (self-regulating sub systems)
Tall organization chart, autocratic style	Flat organization chart, participative style
Competition, gamesmanship	Collaboration, collegiality
Organization's purposes only	Members' and society's purposes also
Alienation	Commitment
Low risk-taking	Innovation

from Trist (1981)

Marine which is critical for Norway's economy. Poorly educated and transient foreign crews could not cope with technically sophisticated ships, and alcoholism was dangerously high. These issues could not have been effectively tackled by any one single company; all firms in the industry, several seafaring unions and a number of maritime regulatory organizations all had to be involved in order to sustain the macro social system development that was required.

The work of Trist and the Tavistock group has been most consistent in applying systems thinking over a large range of sites: the primary work system, the whole organization system and the macro-social domain. In doing so they have illuminated the dynamic nature of organizations and their functioning, the crucial importance of boundary management and the need for a new approach to organizational design which can accommodate environmental change.

BIBLIOGRAPHY

TRIST, E. L., 'The Socio-Technical Perspective', in A. van de Ven and W. F. Joyce (eds.), *Perspectives on Organization Design and Behaviour*, Wiley-Interscience, 1981.

EMERY, F. E., and TRIST, E. L., 'Socio-technical Systems', in C. W. Churchman and M. Verhulst (eds.), *Management Science, Models and Techniques*, vol. 2, Pergamon, 1960; reprinted in F. E. Emery (ed.), *Systems Thinking*, Penguin, 1969.

TRIST, E. L., *et al., Organizational Choice*, Tavistock, 1963.

EMERY, F. E., and TRIST, E. L., 'The Causal Texture of Organizational Environments', *Human Relations* 18 (1965), 21–32; reprinted in F. E. Emery (ed.), *Systems Thinking*, Penguin, 1969.

RICE, A. K., *Productivity and Social Organization*, Tavistock, 1958.

EMERY, F. E., and THORSRUD, E., *Democracy at Work*, Martinus Nijhoff (Leiden), 1976.

HERBST, P. G., *Alternatives to Hierarchies*, Martinus Nijhoff (Leiden), 1976.

SIX

Organizational Change and Learning

. . . we contend, bureaucratization and other forms of organizational change occur as a result of processes which make organizations more similar without necessarily making them more efficient.
PAUL J. DIMAGGIO and WALTER W. POWELL

. . . the real problem of strategic change is ultimately one of managerial process and action; of signalling new areas for concern and anchoring those signals in issues for attention and decision, of mobilizing energy and enthusiasm in an additive fashion to ensure that new problem areas found and defined eventually gain sufficient legitimacy and power to result in contextually appropriate action.
ANDREW PETTIGREW

Organizational defensive routines are anti-learning and over-protective.
CHRIS ARGYRIS

Today's problems come from yesterday's 'solutions'.
PETER SENGE

Imaginization – an invitation to develop new ways of thinking about organization and management – an invitation to re-image ourselves and what we do.
GARETH MORGAN

Organizations do change, whether for better or worse, and writers on organizations have examined the ways in which change comes about. Some have concentrated on the factors in the organization's context and environment which appear both to impel particular changes to occur and also to set constraints for them. Others have underlined that appropriate change which assists the organization to become more effective only comes about through considerable effort on the part of the organization's managers. They have to understand the need for change and be consciously working to achieve it. In addition, modern organizations are in situations which require continuous development. They not only need to change; they have to acquire a capacity for learning.

Paul DiMaggio and Walter Powell argue that organizations change to be more like each other, since the pressures from the state, from other institutions, and from professional standards, require managers to conform to accepted practice. In contrast, Andrew Pettigrew underlines the specific complexity for each organization of the interacting factors of context, content and process with which managers have to grapple to execute an effective strategic change.

Chris Argyris points to the power of 'defensive routines', the psychological blocks to considering change, which limit an organization's ability to draw on the full potential of its members. He suggests ways in which they might be overcome to produce an organization more open to change and able to participate in new learning. Peter Senge is concerned to establish the characteristics of a 'learning organization': i.e. one which, through a systems approach, is able to learn continuously.

Gareth Morgan maintains that understanding an organization is greatly helped by applying a range of different images to it. This 'imaginization' is the key to being better able to conceive of possible changes.

Paul J. DiMaggio and Walter W. Powell

Paul DiMaggio and Walter Powell are American professors of sociology based at Yale and Arizona universities respectively. They are leading exponents of the particular approach to the study and understanding of organizations known as 'Institutional Theory'.

Institutional theory begins from Weber's views on the functioning of bureaucracy (see p. 7). Weber argues that the 'rational legal' bureaucratic type of organizational structure has become dominant in modern society because it is the most efficient form. It is based on rationally calculating how to organize to achieve desired ends. It has a hierarchy of authority, experts who have specific areas of responsibility, and a system of rules, which together control the organization's activities. It uses the files of the 'bureau' to record the past behaviour of the organization and to capture the professionally determined best available knowledge relevant to its goals. It can therefore carry out its activities unambiguously, predictably, continuously and speedily. Since it is efficient, bureaucracy is used by governments needing both to control their staff and citizenry and to give equal protection under the law. It is also used by capitalist business firms who are in competition and therefore need to operate efficiently.

Writers in the first section of this book, like Chandler (see p. 20), Mintzberg (see p. 32) and others, seek to describe and explain different types of organizational structure. But DiMaggio and Powell point out that bureaucracy has spread continuously during the twentieth century, becoming the usual organizational form. They therefore ask not why do organization structures differ, but why is there such an overriding degree of homogeneity in organizational forms and practices? Organizations of the same type in any organizational field (for example, business firms in the same industry, government departments, hospitals) may have displayed considerable diversity in approach when they were first set up. But once a field becomes established there is an inexorable push towards bureaucratic homogeneity.

But, unlike Weber, DiMaggio and Powell question whether this convergence is due to the efficiency of the bureaucratic form, which leads all to strive towards it. Rather, they maintain that the convergence is a result of institutional pressures from the environment on managers in an organizational field to become more similar to one another, *whether this leads to greater efficiency or not*. This emergence of a common structure and approach among organizations in the same field is referred to as *institutional isomorphism*. This is the constraining process which forces one unit in a population to come to resemble those other units that face the same set of environmental conditions. It is important since among the major factors that organizations must respond to are other organizations in their environments. It is through these organizations that managers get their ideas about how to run organizations and obtain legitimacy for the actions which they take. Legitimate actions are those which conform to the common view; they do not have to be effective.

There are three mechanisms through which institutional isomorphism produces conformity: *coercive* isomorphism (which stems from political influence), *mimetic* isomorphism (which results from responses to uncertainty) and *normative* isomorphism (which results from the professionalization of managers and specialists). Each of these mechanisms describes a process by which ideas from institutions in the organization's environment become legitimized and adopted.

Coercive isomorphism results from pressures, both formal and informal, from other important organizations in the environment. These pressures are of various sorts. They may have the force of law as, for example, pollution-control regulations or anti-discrimination legislation. They may come from external institutions, as when government support agencies require certain accounting procedures to be in place before giving their support to charities, or when important customers require particular delivery systems from their suppliers. The pressure may come from internal authority as, for example, in the case of common control information required by the Head Office of a corporation from all its subsidiaries. The pressures may be persuasive in character, but they are still very real, as when standards for school curricula or new products are publicly recommended.

One result of coercive pressures may be that the conformity obtained is only superficial. Indeed, in some cases there may be a general collusion that something is being done rather than actual change taking place. For example, health and safety regulations may ensure that all organizations appoint a specialist officer, but may otherwise allow the issue to be relatively neglected throughout a whole sector. All these institutional pressures act coercively to produce a convergence in structures and procedures.

Mimetic isomorphism is based on imitation. All organizations face uncertainty, having to deal with problems with ambiguous causes and unclear solutions. This leads to what March (see p. 139) has identified as *problemistic search*, i.e. a short-term, short-sighted, simple-minded activity to find ways of dealing with a particularly urgent problem. A common result of such searches is to copy what others in a similar situation are reported to be doing successfully, since this gives legitimation. For example, following their application in a firm generally regarded as successful, new management practices, as propagated by consultants, may then be regarded as legitimate and be taken up by many organizations.

So techniques such as job enrichment or zero-based budgeting, and new philosophies, such as 'excellence' or human resource management, quickly spread. A dramatic example of such imitation is the way in which the concept of quality circles was neglected by US managements, until it proved popular and effective in Japan, when it was then rapidly legitimized and embraced by Western firms. Such imitation may lead to a quick viable solution with less expense. But it is often undertaken when no such benefit is obvious, since being the same as the rest reduces management's feelings of uncertainty and can produce benefits in terms of image. As an example, Powell studied a public television station which, on a consultant's recommendation, switched from a functional structure to a divisional one (see Chandler, p. 20). Station executives were sceptical of any efficiency gains; some services had to be duplicated across divisions, for example. But they adopted the change because they wanted to give the image that the station was becoming more 'business-minded'. Again, all these pressures to imitate foster an organizational conformity.

The third source of environmental pressures towards organizational convergence is that of *normative isomorphism*. This results primarily from the continuing professionalization of the organization's managers and specialists. They wish to demonstrate that they are fully professional and up-to-the-minute in regard to good standards, whether in information technology, accounting requirements or marketing techniques. Having had a common training, professionals are in many ways much closer to their professional counterparts in other organizations than they are to their managerial colleagues in their own. They therefore propagate common norms of legitimate practice which push all organizations to converge.

An important way in which normative isomorphism is encouraged is through the selection of the top personnel of organizations. A filtering often takes place. This might come about through the practice of recruiting high-fliers from a narrow range of training institutions; e.g. Ivy League business schools in the US, *grandes écoles* in France. Another filter comes from promoting to top positions only from a narrow range of specialisms, e.g. financial or legal. Professional careers may themselves be controlled at entry level and at key progression points. All these filters create a pool of individuals in senior jobs with very similar backgrounds, training and experience.

These similarities have been shown among superintendents in a US public school system, and among the Board members of the Fortune top 500 companies. Some entrants to senior jobs are different, having managed to avoid the filters, e.g. black senior officials, women Board members, Jewish naval officers. They are likely to be subjected to considerable persuasive pressures to gain legitimacy by acting in exactly the same way as the others. As before, the results are that the norms practised lead to organizational isomorphism.

These pressures for institutional isomorphism are so considerable, maintain DiMaggio and Powell, that the processes can be expected to continue even in the absence of evidence that the changes increase organizational effectiveness. Indeed, if organizations do become more effective, the reason is often that they are rewarded for their similarity to other organizations in their field. This can make it easier for them to transact business with other organizations, attract professional staff and to be acknowledged as legitimate and respectable – this last being very important to public agencies in attracting financial support. But none of these factors ensure that they are actually more efficient than deviant organizations.

BIBLIOGRAPHY

DIMAGGIO, PAUL J., and POWELL, WALTER W., 'The Iron Cage Revisited: Institutional Isomorphism and Collective Rationality in Organizational Fields', *American Sociological Review*, 48 (1983), 147–60; reprinted in

W. W. Powell and P. J. DiMaggio (eds.), *The New Institutionalism in Organizational Analysis*, University of Chicago Press, 1991; also reprinted in D. S. Pugh (ed.), *Organization Theory*, Penguin, 1997.

POWELL, WALTER W., and DIMAGGIO, PAUL J. (eds.), *The New Institutionalism in Organizational Analysis*, University of Chicago Press, 1991.

Andrew Pettigrew

Andrew Pettigrew is Distinguished Professor of Organizational Behaviour at the University of Warwick Business School, England, where he founded the Centre for Corporate Strategy and Change and was, for many years, its director. The centre has been a leader in strategic change research in Britain. In its work on understanding the processes of change it takes a historical approach which is grounded in a detailed study of the context of an organization in its industrial environment.

Pettigrew maintains that strategic change is a complex, situation-dependent, continuous process. As the diagram shows, it has to be understood in terms of three essential dimensions: context (both internal and external), content (e.g. objectives and assumptions) and process (e.g.

Dimensions for understanding strategic change

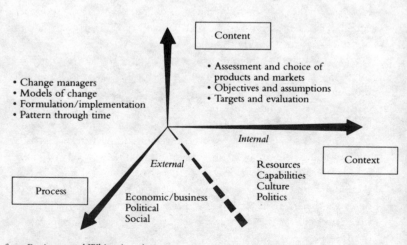

from Pettigrew and Whipp (1991)

implementation patterns). Since management decision-making is a political process, change is inevitably suffused with organizational politics. In major decisions, whoever is powerful among the decision group will determine the outcomes.

The bases of power in organizations may vary. *The Politics of Organizational Decision-Making* is a detailed study of how one decision came to be made: the acquisition of a new computer system by a British chain store. In this decision the technical manager was very powerful. One important source of his power was his ability to understand and to control the information on options which went to the Board. This is an example of a common power base: the emergence of a strong specialization in a then new technology, which reduces the power of the non-specialists. But other bases of power are also available, and what they are have to be examined in each case by studying the management processes in the context in which they take place. No easy generalizations can be made in relating these to the outcome decisions (see Hickson, p. 17).

This focus on the processes of strategic change was continued by Pettigrew in detailed studies of change in a number of divisions of ICI, the then British industrial conglomerate. Change may be viewed as a sequence of four stages, each with its own problems:

1. The development of concern: this involves problem-sensing, leading to legitimizing the notion of change and getting it on the corporate agenda. It is a time-consuming and politically sensitive process, and one in which top management plays a critical role. One of the contributions that leaders of ICI such as Lord Beeching and Sir John Harvey-Jones made was to continually flag up key problems facing ICI which required it to change.

2. Getting acknowledgement and understanding of the problems: the building of a climate of opinion necessary for change was shown to be a long process, requiring many iterations and encountering blocks and unpredictable areas of movement along the way. Major change always affects power structures, career paths and reward systems and is therefore unlikely to be straightforward in its application. In two ICI divisions management training and development were used to equip the managers with the capacity to carry through the operational changes.

3. Planning and acting: it is very important in this stage to have established a desired future state of the organization around which planning can take place and commitment be generated. In one division of ICI this involved giving out clear, simple messages within a broad philosophy of downsizing and reorganization for profitability, and maintaining them without dilution.

4. Stabilizing change: in this stage management needs to ensure that the rewards, information flows and pattern of power and authority support the new position. Since changes are often initiated by key figures, a danger is that they last only as long as these individuals remain in their posts. A key task is thus to ensure continuity by the development and appointment of appropriate successors.

Pettigrew also examined the contribution of the various Organizational Development (OD) groups which were operating in the different divisions of ICI. Their success, and continued existence, varied considerably between the divisions. One chastening lesson is not to expect too much from such OD specialists. As one supportive senior manager put it: 'using OD is in the first case an act of faith'.

In a further study with his colleague Richard Whipp, now of Cardiff Business School, five key problems of managing strategic change were identified. Each of these is complex in itself and, in addition, has to be related to the other four. The problems are:

Assessing the environment;
Leading change;
Linking strategic and operational change;
Treating human resources as assets and as liabilities;
Developing a coherent approach.

These five problem areas are examined in detailed studies of firms attempting to manage strategic change in the British vehicle, book publishing, merchant banking and assurance industries. Among the firms studied were Jaguar, Peugeot Talbot, Longman, Kleinwort Benson, Hill Samuel and the Prudential. For each area there are many factors and mechanisms to be examined, and these are different for each industry and for each firm.

When tackling the first problem, *assessing the environment*, it is not enough for companies to regard this as a technical exercise which can be left to appropriate specialists. Understanding the environment must be regarded as a multifunctional activity in which all top management participates as a continuous learning process. This is because for key firms in an industry there is a large subjective element in which their understanding, and therefore their company's activities, actually determine what the environment will become (see Weick, p. 124). Thus, the understanding of Longman staff as to the nature of their environment led to actions on their part which altered the shape of the book trade and helped to redefine the nature of that market. Again, the change in the 1970s in the way in which the Prudential Assurance company viewed the basis for competitive behaviour in the assurance industry – away from actuarial risk towards product diversification – enabled it to redefine itself as the 'Prudential Corporation'. It was thus better placed to move forward to the structural changes necessary to operate in the changing market.

The second problem, that of *leading change*, is also complex and situation-specific, but done in a series of incremental steps in which many managers are involved. It requires building a climate accepting of change within the firm and, in addition, building the capability to mount the changes. This is quite the opposite of the 'heroic leader' notion of leading change, which is inappropriate. Thus, the regeneration of the car company Peugeot Talbot required the establishment of new, open working relationships among senior management, a reworking of the relations with the parent company, a rebuilding of the confidence of the staff, shell-shocked after earlier major contractions, and the progressive elaboration of a new model programme through improved communications and structures. Such a change from survival to regeneration could not be accomplished by one person or through a single programme. It involved the emergence over a period of years of new leaders both at the top and at lower levels within the company.

The next key problem then becomes the *linking of strategic and operational change*. This is difficult because the implementation of strategic intentions over time inevitably transforms them, and what is done during implementation may overwhelm the original strategy. Indeed, often what are considered as strategies are merely the *post hoc* labelling of what was done: 'that worked, so it was our strategy to do it.' Great attention is required to ensure that operational aspects do not undermine the general strategy. Actionable targets must become the responsibility of change managers operating at many levels. They have to be supported by re-thought communication mechanisms and new reward systems. A major problem is that both strategic and operational change processes have to happen over the same time span and inevitably become 'political' as they press for change and meet opposition.

The problem is highlighted in the contrast between the two merchant banks studied. In the 1970s Kleinwort Benson had begun to sense trends in its environment, to identify the need for strategic development and to foster a commitment to strategic change among senior staff. In the 1980s these capacities allowed the firm to adopt a broad strategic position (the expansion of international banking) and to work to drive the implications of that strategy throughout the organization. It was able to learn from failures (e.g. the slowness of internal deliberations, which led to the failure to purchase a Far Eastern stockbroker), to make compensating changes linked to the strategy. By the time of the deregulation of the British stock market in the 1980s it was able to take relatively swift action, for example, in the acquisition of specialist firms in new activities such as 'interest rate swaps' and 'Eurobonds'.

Hill Samuel, on the other hand, did not construct a fresh corporate strategy in the 1970s: what strategy there was emerged from the amalgam of operational activities, which were continually growing and diversifying. It did not, therefore, develop a capacity to formulate and implement strategy. So in the early 1980s the linking of strategic and operational change was immensely difficult. The gap between the new ideas and the organization's capacity for change was very wide, and the new Chief Executive had to build up linkages personally. Over a period he had some success, but the strategic and operational linkages were still comparatively immature. Thus, the senior management never resolved differences over location, and when the Board offered to sell the company to a Swiss bank, the CE resigned. Although that deal fell through, the firm was then purchased by the TSB, a British bank.

It is vital to regard *human resources as both assets and liabilities* and to take appropriate action. The organization's members must provide the knowledge base for learning, but it is also necessary to undertake 'unlearning' when the established conceptions and skills are no longer appropriate. Shedding outmoded techniques and attitudes is not easy. Jaguar, for example, had to launch a major programme of Human Resource Management (HRM) in the 1980s when it undertook the challenge to become a profitable, high-quality-car manufacturer. It had to move away from the traditional British motor industry's conflict-focused industrial relations view of personnel management. The new HRM approach involved recruiting staff, training staff and developing the commitment of all to the firm's mission. This was done through the use of new specialisms, such as manpower and salary planning, and internal communications services. Schemes for profit-sharing, employee shareholding, and open learning to develop new skills were established. These added up to a very demanding set of changes that needed considerable resources.

And the final problem is that of *coherence*, i.e. the ability to hold the organization together while simultaneously reshaping it. Four elements of strategic thinking are required:

1. Consistency in ensuring that the attempts to tackle existing problems do not contain internal contradictions. For example, earlier in Peugeot Talbot's existence its then owners, Chrysler UK, tried to make it into a high volume car producer although it had not mastered the special production techniques required.
2. Consonance, i.e. that the strategy should be well adapted to the environment. It should not become the victim of the organization's entrenched partial view of its competitive position, as was the case with Hill Samuel.
3. Competitive advantage, i.e. that the strategy aimed for should give comparative advantage in the market. For example, Longman's growth strategy included the market-led decision to add the fields of professional and business publishing to its established strengths in educational publishing.
4. Feasibility of the strategy in the resources needed. This was a problem that Jaguar, for example, had to beware of in its rush for change and growth.

The underlying conclusion of these studies is the recognition of the interconnectedness of all the factors involved. It is not possible to provide a general checklist of dos and don'ts in managing strategic change. Only a full understanding of the situation in each case can identify the course of the changes.

BIBLIOGRAPHY

PETTIGREW, A., *The Politics of Organizational Decision-Making*, Tavistock, 1973.

PETTIGREW, A., *The Awakening Giant: Continuity and Change in ICI*, Blackwell, 1985.

PETTIGREW, A., 'Context and Action in the Transformation of the Firm', *Journal of Management Studies*, 1987, 24, 649–70; reprinted in D. S. Pugh (ed.), *Organization Theory*, Penguin, 1997.

PETTIGREW, A., and WHIPP, R., *Managing Change for Competitive Success*, Blackwell, 1991.

Chris Argyris

Chris Argyris is a psychologist who has for many years been James Bryant Conant Professor of Education and Organizational Behaviour at Harvard University, where he is now Professor Emeritus. He began his career at Yale University, and his important contributions to the field have been recognized with the establishment at that university of a Chair named in his honour: the Chris Argyris Chair in the Social Psychology of Organizations.

Argyris has consistently studied the ways in which the personal development of individuals is affected by the kind of situation in which they work. Each person has a potential which, if fully realized, would bring benefits not only to the individual but also to the working group and employing organization. Unfortunately, businesses and other organizations are usually run in such a way that such benefits are prevented from appearing.

This is because the typical approach of the managements of organizations and their lack of interpersonal competence prevent people from becoming mature in outlook. Employees too often remain short-sighted in their actions on the job, shirking responsibility and being uninterested in opportunities.

They develop 'defensive routines' which protect their current ways of working and inhibit them from considering any changes – even changes that would improve their present position. In their limited routine tasks they look forward to the end of the day's work, but are unable to foresee the success or failure of the whole enterprise over a period of years. To their superiors their infuriating inability to see beyond the end of their noses and their own relatively trivial work difficulties are inexplicable. They have come to accept a passive and dependent position, without initiative.

Faced with this lack of response, even among lower managers or specialists, executives are liable to become yet more autocratic and directive.

Their existing strong 'pyramidal values' are reinforced. The increased use of management controls deprives employees of any opportunity of participating in the important decisions which affect their working life, leading to feelings of psychological failure. It is not they themselves but control systems (such as work study and cost accounting) which define, inspect and evaluate the quality and quantity of their performance. And as subordinates tell less and less about what is happening, as everyone pays more attention to keeping up appearances ready for the next business process re-engineering investigation or tense budget allocation committee meeting, so defensive routines come to be the norm.

These are some of the problems human beings have in relating to organizational life. Together with Donald A. Schon, Argyris has also examined some of the built-in contradictions that arise from the functioning of the organization itself, which has the paradoxical requirement of both wanting to maintain stability and also be dynamic or changing. Thus, typically, organization members may be told: take initiatives *but* do not violate rules; think beyond the present *but* be rewarded and penalized on present performance only; think of the organization as a whole *but* do not cross into others' areas of responsibility; cooperate with others *but* compete with others when required.

The main problem is not that these contradictions exist, but that in the usual poor state of managerial interpersonal competence, they cannot be raised and discussed as issues. Although many managers may *talk* about the openness of communication and the participative approach of their organizations (what is called their 'espoused' theory), what they actually do may be very different. There are very strong defensive routines built into many managements' thinking, ensuring that they resist the openness which leads to interpersonal change.

Argyris and Schon have demonstrated that the basis of many managers' actions (called their 'theory-in-use') can be subsumed under four rules of behaviour, referred to as Model I: (i) design goals unilaterally and try to achieve them, (ii) maximize winning and minimize losing by controlling the task with as little dependence on others as possible, (iii) minimize generating or expressing negative feelings in public, keep your own thoughts and feelings a mystery, (iv) be rational and 'objective' and suppress the voicing of feelings by others, thus protecting yourself and them from facing important issues which often have an emotional content to them.

Managers who operate on Model I have a very unilateral view of their world, in which they are striving to have complete control. Their aim is to defend themselves and impose on others. They thus generate mistrust and rigidity and are therefore confirmed in their Model I view that open discussion of issues is best avoided. The only learning that occurs is learning how to conform (called 'single-loop' learning) and the process becomes 'self-sealing'.

Argyris and Schon propose a Model II theory-in-use which does allow organizational learning. The norms here are: (i) take action on valid information and be open about obtaining it, (ii) take action after free and informed choice with all who are competent and relevant taking part, (iii) generate internal commitment to the choice with monitoring of implementation and preparedness to change. Managers who operate in a Model II world are not defensive and thus they can participate in 'double loop' learning. They look for contributions from others who are competent; they are able to confront their own basic assumptions and take part in testing them in public, which allows of their changing.

The issue then becomes: if managers operating in a Model I 'mode' are by definition unaware of this fact since they are using defensive routines to resist change, how may they be helped to develop effective learning in Model II? Argyris proposes a training programme to bring out into the open these contradictions, in situations where managers' feelings of vulnerability are reduced. Managers are helped by interpersonal consultants to confront the large gap which usually exists between what is said and done in a decision-making group and what is actually felt by the members. They can then analyse the defensive routines which they habitually use to stop openness and innovation and practise taking a Model II approach in their work.

Using this approach, Argyris conducted a case study lasting over five years, as described in his book *Knowledge for Action*. It was both a consulting and a research programme – a combination known as 'action research'. He worked with the owner-directors of a management consultancy firm to develop their Model II skills. He shows that his seminars helped them to overcome their defensive routines on many occasions (not all). Inevitably, some managers became more competent at Model II behaviour than others. Often in change programmes it is found that top managers put the need for change high in their espoused theory, but their theory-in-use stays the same. Unusually, in this case it was the senior managers who made the most progress. They are at the forefront of making the firm better capable of organizational learning.

BIBLIOGRAPHY

ARGYRIS, C., *Personality and Organization*, Harper & Row, 1957.

ARGYRIS, C., *Organization and Innovation*, Irwin, 1965.

ARGYRIS, C., and SCHON, D., *Organizational Learning: A Theory of Action Perspective*, Addison-Wesley, 1978.

ARGYRIS, C., *Strategy, Change and Defensive Routines*, Pitman, 1985.

ARGYRIS, C., *Knowledge for Action: A Guide to Overcoming Barriers to Change*, Jossey-Bass, 1993.

Peter Senge

Peter Senge is a systems theorist who is Director of the Systems Thinking and Organizational Learning Programme of the Sloan School of Management at the Massachusetts Institute of Technology. He argues that in the present-day, complex world organizations have to be able to learn how to cope with continuous change in order to be successful; i.e. they have to become *learning organizations*. His concern is to describe the art and practice of such a learning organization.

It is not easy for organizations to learn because they are afflicted with learning disabilities, such as:

Excessive commitment of individuals to their own positions. This limited view leads to people focusing only on their own role and taking little responsibility for the results produced when all the positions interact.

Blame is always allocated externally, away from the immediate group: the enemy is out there. It may be other departments (marketing and manufacturing mutually blaming each other), or government regulations, or unfair competition from another country. But blaming external factors hampers learning and is almost always not the complete story.

The illusion of taking charge. Being 'proactive' rather than 'reactive' is attractive to managers, but could simply mean fighting the enemy out there in the same way but more aggressively. Without analysis reflecting on the internal changes necessary, it may simply be disguised reactiveness.

Focusing on immediate events as explanations. This precludes seeing the longer-term patterns of change that lie behind the events and attempting to understand the causes of those larger patterns.

Being unaware of slow, gradual processes that present greater threats than immediate events. It is said that a frog placed in boiling water will immediately jump out but, if placed in warm water which is gradually heated to boiling, will stay and boil, since its sensing apparatus is geared to sudden changes, not to gradual ones. Senge argues that something of the same sort happened to the American motor industry from the mid-1960s to the mid-1980s in regard to Japanese and German competition. Over two decades the latter's share of the market rose from near zero to 38 per cent before US manufacturers took it seriously.

The delusion that learning comes only from experience. We do learn from experience, but in a complex system we can no longer directly experience the consequences of many of our important decisions. Decisions on investment in Research and Development or on strategic positioning may have large ramifications over a decade or more. It is not therefore possible to learn only on the basis of trial and error.

The myth of top management being agreed and united. This leads to suppression of disagreements and encourages watered-down compromises to maintain the appearance of a cohesive team. If disagreement does come to the surface it is expressed in polarized terms with those involved finding fault and blaming each other. Thus, as Argyris (p. 201) shows, real 'double-loop' learning does not take place.

To combat these considerable disabilities Senge proposes five disciplines that organizations need to practise to become learning organizations.

The first concerns *personal mastery*. Individuals need to exercise the highest levels of mastery, not over other people, but over themselves. They need to have a good understanding of themselves and what they wish to achieve. This is the personal learning which is the basis for organizational learning, since no organization's capacity for learning can be greater than that of its members. But few organizations encourage such self-discipline, with the result that there are vast untapped resources of energy and learning potential in organizations.

The second discipline necessitates the continual challenge and review of the deeply entrenched, tacit *mental models* that members of the organization bring to all its activities. Stereotypes of customer behaviour, accepted recipes for product development and the neglect of the possibilities of discontinuous change are examples of mental models that have to be continuously reviewed in an effort to make thinking more open to a wider range of new ideas. The Anglo-Dutch Shell oil company attributes its considerable success over the last two decades in the unpredictable world oil business, to its ability to challenge the mental models of its managers.

The third discipline concerns the *building of a shared vision* for the organization and its members of the future that they wish to create. A shared vision has been the key to all successful organizations: the 'value driven' nature of excellent organizations, as Peters and Waterman put it (p. 114). It has to be more than the usual artificial 'vision statement', a genuine vision of what they want to achieve, which firms such as Ford, IBM, Polaroid and Apple computers have displayed.

The fourth discipline is a commitment to *team learning*: an open dialogue of cooperation in groups, rather than 'turf battles'. Only then can the intelligence of the team exceed that of its members rather than reduce it drastically.

The discipline which unites the others and brings all together in a pattern which can be understandable is that of *systems thinking*. This is the fifth discipline, which provides the title for Senge's book, and is the foundation for organizational learning. It is necessary to think in a systems way which is rather different from our usual focus on immediate events.

There are a number of laws of systems thinking, of which the first is: 'today's problems come from yesterday's "solutions".' Often problems arise from 'solutions' which merely shift the problem to another part of the system. A solution to the problem of high stock inventory that involved drastic reductions might result in salesmen spending large amounts of their time pacifying irate customers awaiting late deliveries. The impounding by the police of a large shipment of drugs may result in an increase of drug-related crime as the reduced availability forces the price up and thus increases the crime levels of addicts desperate to maintain their supply. So other laws of the fifth discipline are 'the harder you push, the harder the system pushes back,' 'the easy way out usually leads back in,' and 'the cure can be worse than the disease.'

A more sophisticated understanding of how complex systems work is required, and managers need training to encourage systems thinking. Another law of the fifth discipline is that 'behaviour grows better before it grows worse.' Treating the symptoms may bring temporary relief, but at the cost of later, larger problems. There is a fundamental mismatch between the behaviour of complex systems and our ways of thinking about them. This is because for important issues 'cause and effect are not closely related in time and space.' The results of a decision taken now may have effects only after some time and in a different part of the organization anyway. Thus, the decision to cut the budget of the training department in a particular year may seem a sensible economy. But in the following year the result might be a large decrease in the operational efficiency of a new computer billing system through inadequate preparation.

The basic contribution of the fifth discipline of systems thinking is the art of seeing the wood *and* the trees. Managers do not often take the time to step back from the trees to see the wood and, unfortunately, when they do step back they just see lots of trees! Senge analyses the sad story of the Peoples' Express Airlines, an innovative, low-cost, high-quality airline ser- vice in the Eastern US, to illustrate the necessity for systems thinking. The airline was founded in 1980 and was immediately successful, growing in five years to become the fifth largest carrier in the USA. But in 1986 it was taken over by another airline, having made a loss of $133 million in the first six months of that year.

What went wrong? Many theories were proposed, including a too great 'people orientation' by the management, lack of an adequate strategy in relation to takeovers, an innovative seat-reservation system introduced by other airlines which allowed price competition, etc. But each of these theories is only partial. A proper analysis requires consideration of the interactions of five sets of factors (air fleet, human resources, competition, finance and policy levers), which generates a list of over forty variables which must be considered in a system-wide way. A simulation was built at MIT which allows many of the variables to be changed to evaluate their impact on the system as a whole. Working with simulation suggests that what is required is an organization which is capable of self-analysis: for example, in understanding that you cannot innovate with dramatically new ideas in human resource policies *and* become a major player in the airline industry within a few years. A firm can grow too fast and so not be able to learn to understand and manage the turbulent changes involved and thus think and act systemically.

A key contribution to an organization's capacity to learn is thus the use of computer-based simulations, called 'microworlds'. These allow for 'play' in developing a more complex systemic understanding of the organ- ization's position and what the possibilities for change are. This leads to the realization of another of the laws of the fifth discipline: 'you can have your cake and eat it too – but not at once.'

BIBLIOGRAPHY

SENGE, P. N., *The Fifth Discipline: The Art and Practice of the Learning Organization*, Century Business, 1992.

SENGE, P. N., 'Mental Models', *Planning Review*, 20 (1992), 4–10, 44; reprinted in D. S. Pugh (ed.), *Organization Theory*, Penguin, 1997.

Gareth Morgan

Born in Wales, Gareth Morgan lives and works in Canada. He is Distinguished Research Professor at York University, Toronto, having moved there from the University of Lancaster in England. He has written books and many articles analysing organizations and management and has been consultant and seminar leader to numerous organizations.

Everyone in an organization has in mind an implicit picture of that organization, a mental image of what it is like. Morgan contends not only that an organization is seen differently by different people, but that it can be seen in different ways by any one person. If multiple images of an organization are used, much greater understanding is gained, for organizations are many things at once, so multiple images envisage more of what is going on. They can reveal new ways of managing and designing organizations that were not apparent before.

Morgan himself puts forward eight possible images of organizations: as machines, as living organisms, as brains, as cultures, as political systems, as psychic prisons, as systems in flux and transformation and as instruments of domination. The name of each image is a metaphor likening an organization to something else and, by doing so, opening up a fresh way of thinking about it.

If an organization is thought of as a *machine*, the emphasis is on the orderly arrangement of who does what and who has authority over whom. This is a mechanical kind of thinking concerned with clear hierarchy, authority and responsibility, discipline, stability and equitable treatment of personnel. It is extolled by classic management theorists such as Fayol and Taylor (see p. 97 and p. 102) and analysed by sociologists such as Weber and Burns (p. 7 and p. 53). The strength of an organization seen and set up in this form is that it works well where a machine would work well, that is, where tasks are straightforward and repetitive, as in a fast-food hamburger chain or an accounts office. Its limitation is that it dehumanizes work.

However, if an organization is seen as a living *organism*, a biological metaphor, then there is less preoccupation with orderliness and more attention is given to adaptiveness. Tasks and lines of authority can be changed to continuously realign the organization responsively with its changing environment. This view is extolled by Peters and by Kanter (p. 111 and p. 118). It is the organic type described by Burns (p. 53) and one of those described by Mintzberg (p. 32). Its strength is that it fosters an organization which is an open, flexible system, giving full scope to human capacities, especially appropriate to competitive and turbulent conditions, as in the aerospace and micro-electronics industries. Its limitations are that it can overlook its own built-in conflict potential, and that, as 'population ecologists' such as Hannan and Freeman (p. 82) have argued, an organization is not infinitely adaptable but can become obsolete and 'die'.

An image of an organization as a *brain* does not mean that it has central planning teams or a research department. Rather, it presumes that intelligence is spread throughout the organization. In this the brain is similar to a holograph, in which any part can reproduce the whole and stand for it. So in all its parts the organization does not just learn, but can learn to learn better. There can be 'double-loop learning' (Argyris, p. 201) that goes further than 'single-loop' learning (which only corrects errors) into another feedback loop that questions the operating norms, the ways of working, that lead to error in the first place. Such an organization would accept uncertainty and self-criticism and be able to see further than the 'bounded rationality' postulated by Simon and by March (p. 134 and p. 137). Were an organization to have a rigid structure, these advantages unfortunately might not be realized. Such a structure would have opposing assumptions embedded in it. It would have specialist departments, each holding on to its own specialized information, each unable to learn from the others or to question its own ways of working.

Seeing an organization in terms of *cultures*, Morgan's fourth image, brings to attention not only its overall corporate culture, but the sub-cultures of its constituent sections and groups and the societal culture of which its own culture is a part. People who share a culture interpret situations and events in similar ways, sustaining their common outlook with evocative figures of speech, symbols and ceremonies. As an obvious instance, even an empty room symbolizes what is expected, having either ordered chairs and notepads or, alternatively, chairs arranged casually. This cultural view reveals the wide organizational life that is beyond the overtly rational, and shows possibilities of change. Even the relationships of an organization with its environment can be reinterpreted, re-thought, and thus changed, as when a railway switches from thinking about passengers, or a hospital about patients, and each begins to think about customers instead.

The fifth image recognizes an organization as a *political system*. An organization can be autocratic or democratic, or anywhere in between. There are departmental interests, management interests and the interests of those lower down, personal career interests, and many more. All interests have a potential for conflict and for wheeling and dealing. They exploit both the legitimate authority classified by Weber (p. 7) and the power drawn from controlling resources and know-how analysed by Pfeffer and Salancik (p. 71) and Hickson (p. 17). The strength of this image is that it helps people to accept the reality of organizational politics and to ask whose interests are being served.

Organizations give purpose and structure to the lives of their members. Our roles become our realities, as Morgan puts it. There lies the danger. For individuals can believe they are more in control than is really the case. In this they deceive themselves. For they can be in a *psychic prison*, attributing to the organization an existence and power of its own and allowing their thinking to be confined by it. Their thinking may indeed be the result of forces in their unconscious, as psychoanalysis has shown. The strength of this prison image is that it exposes how people can become trapped in this way in a certain psychic reality and suggests to them that it is possible to break out of it. Managers can see that their organization is of their own making and take a fresh look at what they are doing.

To see an organization as in constant *flux and transformation*, a seventh possible image, is to see it as being just like everything else in the universe. There are various conceptions of how change takes place. It can be seen as brought about through one-way cause and effect or – and this is better – by mutual causality, in which 'causes' loop back upon themselves. Or by 'autopoiesis', whereby the organization changes itself by changing its own environment. Or by dialectical change, whereby any phenomenon generates its opposite, as when the power of the employers led to the formation of trade unions. This image warns against an organization being seen as struggling against the environment. Rather, it must survive in interdependence with others in that environment.

Finally, Morgan draws a picture of organizations as *instruments of domination*. He points out that the building of the Great Pyramid in Egypt was both a triumph of skill and effort *and* a sacrifice of the labour and lives of many to glorify a few. Organizations achieve much, but as they do so they can cripple people by accidents, diseases and stress. They can abruptly dispose of them after years of service and pollute their habitat. The strength of this image is its recognition that domination of the many by the few is intrinsic to the very concept of hierarchy which exists in virtually every organization.

Morgan shows how the problems of a small firm in the public relations industry may be illuminated by using a range of metaphors. The firm was founded by two senior partners (holding 80 per cent of the equity between them) and two junior partners. It was immediately successful, based on the client centred, all-round competences of the founders in giving a creative service. New staff, when recruited, were encouraged to develop their overall generalist skills, as well as their specializations. While this was time-consuming and expensive, it did give great flexibility to the firm and allowed greater work interest for the staff. There was high commitment and all worked hard and for long hours. Its success allowed the firm to grow in a few years to 150 staff.

Major conflicts began when the senior partners, feeling that the demands of the organization were too great in view of their family commitments, suggested a change to a more formalized structure. Their proposals included job definitions, set procedures for the change of staff between projects, greater control over when staff were away from the office, and in general 'more system'. The junior partners objected that the firm was successful precisely because of the present 'creative chaos' and they saw no need for change. They offered to take more of the workload from the senior partners in exchange for more equity participation in the company. But the senior partners were not prepared to relinquish control in this way. In the event, in spite of the convention that the partners operated by consensus, the senior partners installed the changes. They appeared to be accepted, but within a year the junior partners had left to found their own agency in the original 'creative chaos' style. The firm continued, but less successfully, in that its work was now regarded by some clients as 'sound but uninspiring'.

Several of the metaphors may be used to help to make sense of these developments. The *machine* metaphor would point to the increasing bureaucratization and ask what should be the appropriate level of 'system' in view of the size and dependence of the firm. The living *organism* metaphor would focus on the potential incongruence of the organization in its environment and ask whether it has the degree of creative chaos to be successful in its market niche. The *brain* metaphor would note the loss of the holographic character of the enterprise and ask how far it is now constrained to 'single-loop learning'. The *culture* metaphor would lead to asking how far the values of the original culture have changed, and whether there are ways of re-creating some of those characteristics in the new situation.

Using the *political* system metaphor points to the considerable differences in power between the partners which allowed the senior partners to impose their own decision when real conflicts appeared. What are the limitations on the organization's processes when this degree of power can be exercised? The *psychic prison* metaphor focuses on the psychological factors shaping relationships, including the senior partners' (probably unconscious) need for dominance and the junior partners' (probably equally unconscious) need to resist.

An important benefit of using a range of metaphors is that they supply competing explanations. Proposals for change from one may be tested against another. For example, if the changes in the company were generated by the owners' unconscious need for control, then the underlying problems cannot be solved by addressing only the issues of corporate culture or learning capacity (see Argyris, p. 199).

Managers can apply these ideas, says Morgan, by *imaginization*. This is 'an invitation to re-image ourselves and what we do'. In a book with this title, Morgan illustrates what he means and how he uses images in his own work as a consultant 'to create new momentum in stuck situations'.

It is a book full of lively cartoons and images, from yoghurt pots to lions. One of them 'imaginizes' an organization as a spider plant. This is a plant which throws out long trailing stems, each with a miniature on its end of the original plant. Managers seeing their organization in this way come up with ideas that they have not considered before. One would be that expansion can be by setting up offshoots instead of by increasing the size of the central plant pot. But then what financial support should these new subsidiaries receive? If the organization already has a dispersed form, this image might prompt them to ask whether the central pot is doing enough? Or too much? Are some offshoots withering and becoming a drain on the centre? And so on. Different images raise different questions and so expose problems or opportunities that might otherwise be overlooked.

BIBLIOGRAPHY

MORGAN, G., *Images of Organization*, Sage, 1986.
MORGAN, G., *Imaginization: The Art of Creative Management*, Sage, 1993.

Name Index

Subject Index